THE 12 DISCIPLES OF GREAT MEN

DIVINE PRINCIPLES FOR PERSONAL SPIRITUAL AND BUSINESS SUCCESS EXPOSED

By

J. U. Passion

© Copyright 2020 by iPromosmedia LLC - All rights reserved.

It is not legal to reproduce, duplicate, or transmit any part of this document in either electronic means or printed format. Any recording of this publication is strictly prohibited.

ISBN: 978-1-7352896-0-1 (Hardcover)

ISBN: 978-1-7352896-1-8 (eBook)

ISBN: 978-1-7352896-2-5 (Paperback)

Global Version

THE HOLY BIBLE, NEW INTERNATIONAL VERSION®, NIV® Copyright © 1973, 1978, 1984, 2011 by Biblica, Inc.® Used by permission. All rights reserved worldwide.

Scripture taken from the New King James Version®. Copyright © 1982 by Thomas Nelson. Used by permission. All rights reserved.

Scripture quotations taken from the 21st Century King James Version®, copyright © 1994. Used by permission of Deuel Enterprises, Inc., Gary, SD 57237. All rights reserved.

"Scripture quotations taken from the New American Standard Bible® (NASB),

Copyright © 1960, 1962, 1963, 1968, 1971, 1972, 1973,

1975, 1977, 1995 by The Lockman Foundation

"Scripture quotations taken from the Amplified® Bible (AMP),

Copyright © 2015 by The Lockman Foundation

"Scripture quotations taken from the Amplified® Bible (AMPC),

Copyright © 1954, 1958, 1962, 1964, 1965, 1987 by The Lockman Foundation

Used by permission. www. Lockman. org"

The Holy Bible, English Standard Version (ESV) is adapted from the Revised Standard Version of the Bible, copyright Division of Christian Education of the National Council of the Churches of Christ in the U.S.A. All rights reserved.

Scripture quotations marked NLT are taken from the Holy Bible, New Living Translation, copyright © 1996, 2004, 2015 by Tyndale House Foundation. Used by permission of Tyndale House Publishers, Inc., Carol Stream, Illinois 60188. All rights reserved.

The Living Bible copyright © 1971 by Tyndale House Foundation. Used by permission of Tyndale House Publishers Inc., Carol Stream, Illinois 60188. All rights reserved. The Living Bible, TLB, and the Living Bible logo are registered trademarks of Tyndale House Publishers.

Good News Translation® (Today's English Version, Second Edition) Copyright © 1992 American Bible Society. All rights reserved.

Amazon Empire: The Rise and Reign of Jeff Bezos (full film) | FRONTLINE PBS | Official. https://www.youtube.com/watch?v=RVVfJVj5z8s

Why Comedian Dave Chappelle Walked Away From $50 million | The Oprah Winfrey Show | OWN - https://www.youtube.com/watch?v=tlScX2stRuo

Mark Zuckerberg at Startup School 2013- Y Combinator
https://www.youtube.com/watch?v=MGsalg2f9js&t=1461s

Table of Contents

Dedication ix
Foreword xi
Preface xiii
    Who am I? xiii
    My Life's Purpose and Destiny xiv
Section I 1
01 Introduction 1
    Great Men Defined 1
02 Choice, Selection & Election 5
    Natural Selection Laws 5
    Faith and Sight 6
    Faith Redefined 8
    Divine Election by Grace 8
    God Elected Pharaoh 10
    Balance in Nature 10
03 All Men are Created Equal but Unique 13
    Every Man Has Treasures Embedded in Them 13
    Mentorship vs Discipleship 14
    Virtual Discipleship 15
    Life is All About Selling 16
    Fishing vs Evangelism and Marketing 16
    Section Summary 17
12 General Qualities of Greatness 19
SECTION II 23
The 12 Disciples' Positive Values & Principles 23

Chapter 01	25
The Boldness of Peter	25
Become a Voice to the Voiceless	25
Take Monumental Risks	26
Learn How to Deal with Failure	27
Stop Complaining and Murmuring	28
Forgive the Past and Move-On	28
Improvise, Improvise, Improvise	29
Invent New Products, Ideas and Solutions	29
Abandon Distractions	30
Sacrifice Your Wealth	31
Sacrifice Your Time	32
Solve Problems Around You	33
Be as Bold as a Lion	33
Be Persistent	34
Chapter Summary	36
Chapter 02	37
The Smartness of Andrew	37
You Should Always Be Alert	37
Avoid Procrastination	38
Avoid Illegal Deals	39
Study and Learn Daily	39
Avoid Ignorance	41
Greatness Is Not Taught in College	41
Drop Out If College Interferes	42
Discover Your Talents Early	43
Grab New Opportunities like Jeff Bezos	44

Offer Free Services Like Facebook & Google 44

Chapter Summary 46

Chapter 03 47

The Thunder of James 47

Publicly Denounce and Criticize Immorality 48

Promote Nonviolence 49

Allow Due Process 50

Unleash Prayer as Your Spiritual Weapon 51

Chapter Summary 52

Chapter 04 53

The Dependability of John 53

Learn to Be Reliable 54

Keep All Secrets Secret 54

Accept Civic Responsibilities 55

Chapter Summary 55

Chapter 05 57

The Practicality of Philip 57

Avoid Bad Compulsive Behavior 57

Work Better with Numerical Data 58

Set Realizable Goals 59

Chapter Summary 60

Chapter 06 61

The Integrity of Nathanael 61

Do Not Tell Lies, It Belittles You 61

Be Honest with Money; Pay Your Tax 62

Be Positively Predictable 64

Be Morally Correct 65

    Chapter Summary 66
Chapter 07 67
The Skepticism of Thomas 67
    Think for Yourself 68
    Create and Apply A Skeptic-Filter 68
    Question and Fact-Check Everything 68
    Do Not Believe the Internet 69
    Do Not Trust Every News on TV 70
    Get Daily Reports 70
    Apply Selective Lifestyle Formula 71
    Chapter Summary 71
Chapter 08 73
The Discipline of Matthew 73
    Adopt a Disciplined Life 74
    Avoid Discrimination and Segregation 74
    Disregard Beauty for Character 75
    Chapter Summary 75
Chapter 09 77
The Anonymity of James 77
    Great men Prefer to Remain Anonymous 77
    Do Not Be Boastful 78
    Practice Selflessness 79
    Chapter Summary 79
Chapter 10 81
The Zeal of Jude 81
    Develop Passion for Your Society 81
    Be Diligent in Your Work 83

Become a Man of Hope 84
Aspire and Become a Man of Faith 85
Embrace Optimism 86
Exercise Some Patience 86
Pay Attention to Detail 87
Focus on Your Life's Purpose & Destiny 87
Develop a Passion for Service to Customers 89
Chapter Summary 89

Chapter 11 91
The Patriotism of Simon 91
Love Your Nation & People 91
Go Vote and Be Voted For 92
Fight for Equal Rights & Justice 94
Chapter Summary 95

Chapter 12 97
The Frugality of Judas 97
Avoid The 'Love' of Money 97
Delay Gratification (Dave Chappelle Style) 98
Stop Wastefulness 99
Do Not Support Abusive Habits 99
Take Control Over Money 100
Live Above Debt 100
Budget, Budget, Budget 101
Put Money Last 101
Chapter Summary 102

Conclusion 103
About the Author 105

Other Books by The Author... 106

Dedication

I dedicate this book to you, the reader
for that singular effort and desire, to learn about greatness,
and the bold action to select this book
as a guide.

Foreword

You, Too, Can Be Great!

The 12 Disciples of Great Men is a motivational must-read for those who desire to learn strategies on how to become an effective change agent in these last days. Pastor J. U. Passion lays out a blueprint for men and women to follow if they are to fulfill their God given assignment upon the earth. This book is a combination of common sense and divine revelation. The author uses imagery to help the reader understand powerful concepts such as the benefit of being persistent. As you read the 12 Disciples of Great Men, the handwriting on the wall becomes crystal clear. Like a GPS, this book allows you to locate yourself and then guides you to your pre-ordained destination. What makes this book valuable is how Mr. Passion helps you to understand what to do and what not to do.

Oftentimes, on our quest to become great we are snagged by pitfalls simply because we were not warned of the possible dangers ahead. This book is a comprehensive guide that addresses the highs and lows of the journey to greatness. Be ready to challenge your belief system about education versus learning. Once you assess your reasons behind your pursuit of a higher education, you just may be surprised that it may not be a prerequisite to your success and destiny.

Pastor Passion focuses on what you do have instead of what you do not have. Self-investment and self-development are necessary actions and vital steps in discovering your life's purpose. This book lends itself to practical advice that is taken from the lives of the twelve disciples of Christ. Characteristics such as boldness, smartness, thunder, dependability, practicality, integrity, skepticism, discipline, zeal, patriotism, and frugality are essential in the development of your personal, spiritual and business successes.

The 12 Disciples of Great Men gives those aspiring to greatness hope and a plan to get there. This is a refreshing read embedded with realistic instructions and expectations.

As you may know, the road to greatness can sometimes be ugly, lonely, challenging, and layered with difficulties. Mr. Passion admonishes the reader to employ the roadmap to greatness with confidence and humility. The 12 Disciples of Great Men is filled with practical wisdom that when applied will achieve divine greatness. This book is a reflection of who I have come to know of Pastor Juddie Passion. As soon as we met and began to share our beliefs, it was confirmed that he has much to share with society. Coming from the continent of Africa into the United States of America has given him opportunities to explore the principles he shares in this book.

Pastor J. U. Passion's style of writing is simple enough for grade school pupils to understand; yet, the concepts he elaborates on are relevant and applicable in the 21st century. In my role as a financial coach, I can attest to the advice he gives in reference to handling business and customer service with a heart of integrity. I have come to know that he is a great man who strives to fulfill his purpose by exercising and developing each character trait mentioned. You will be enlightened and empowered as you read the pages of this book. I admonish you to study it and put the lessons to use as you pursue your own destiny of becoming GREAT!

- **Pamela Denise Nicholson**
Teacher & Equity Liaison at Broward Public Schools
Licensed Representative with PFS Investments, Inc.
Author of Behind the Stained-Glass Windows

Preface

Who am I?

I was born in 1974 as the first child into a humble family out there in the 'outermost-part-of-the-earth' in Africa to my Christian parents who were elders in our local church. My father (now late) was a steadfast preacher of the gospel and my mother is a deaconess. I was raised in the church so-to-speak; that means no extra social life other than school and church activities.

When I was grown, **I tried many things but lost interest in all of them** including becoming a soldier in the US Army and the French Foreign Legion, electronics, computers, and programming, etc. I wanted to become a strongman in the world; a soldier, hero, or private investigator mostly after watching so many action movies. Movie heroes like Rambo, Commando, Jackie Chan, Chuck Norris, Bruce Lee, etc. fascinated me. I now understand **God wants me to become a great man in the kingdom of Heaven** and not in the world. **God has pre-ordained me to become the voice to the voiceless, food to the hungry, home to the homeless, emancipator to the oppressed and divine health to the sick.**

I began to preach as a Minister in 2017. By this time, I was weary of secular life and aspirations because I could not become the strongman I wanted to be. The inspirations, revelations, and visions never stopped since when I was a child reading the bible daily. I used to write my revelations on my bible pages as I read them when the Holy Spirit would open my spiritual eyes to a deeper understanding of a verse. I have so many physical notebooks that I write most of my revelations and visions and online documents since when I began using the mobile phone and computers. I have only been genuinely interested in writing and publishing my sermons, revelations, and visions as books because I always receive divine inspiration about several topics and the unction to write and publish them. At the writing of this book, I have a backlog of topics to write about that I have to wake up and fulfill.

After learning so much about Jesus, Dr. Martin Luther King Jr., Mandela, and the rest of the great men who became a sacrificial lamb and fought for the emancipation of humans from oppressors, I visualize myself stepping into their shoes soon. It is this urge that led to the writing of this book and a few that will follow. The inspiration for the 12 Disciples of Great men came to me while I was busy at my day job at Amazon Fulfillment Center. It started with the mystery in the selection of Peter the fisherman to become a fisher-of-men for Jesus. The Holy Spirit then took me through the similarities between the traditional process of fishing, Jesus' ministry and evangelism to business marketing and recruitment procedures.

I could then understand Jesus had the power to work alone if he wanted to, but he recruited ordinary men to help him, so they can carry on when he would eventually go back to Heaven. I could satisfy my curiosity why Jesus selected ordinary men with faults and strange characters into his team. Looking up to Jesus as a great man, I could deduct from his person some values that makes him extraordinary and now I relate those values to living men and how anyone can become a great man just like Jesus did by discovering, developing and deploying these values in their personal, spiritual and business lives.

My Life's Purpose and Destiny

Since the encounter, I have constantly been trying to polish my life to fit into the shoes of Jesus Christ, M L K, Mandela etc., as a great man. This knowledge has helped me in my quest to becoming the great man I always dreamt to become. In my brief sojourn in the universe, I have seen so much oppression and inequality across ages and continents while no one dares to fight for the poor for fear of persecution. I wish to become that great man who will stand up for the oppressed and fight for their emancipation by applying nonviolence as taught by Jesus Christ (using prayer as a means of spiritual warfare).

In my quest for the meaning of life, I found out that **life becomes more meaningful when we become of service to other people** in the society and I question myself every time saying:

What am I doing for other people?

What are my contributions to the society?

What are my contributions to the Kingdom of heaven?

These questions bother me daily. That is why I have put my talents to work by writing books from divine inspiration for everyone to read and change their lives for good. I implore you to ask yourself the same question, "Are you doing anything for anyone or are you just being selfish?"

Martin Luther King Jr. is asking you the same question too and says, "Life's most persistent and urgent question is: What are you doing for others?" Hiding in your mothers' closet from the world is not the answer. Timidity can never help another man. Fear of the unknown will never help the oppressed in this society. **The fear of your actual person and your future should not intimidate you, but energize and challenge you to use your talents to help in the society as a great man.** This book will challenge you and give you the facts to become a great man by utilizing the talents that are inbuilt in you. Take this word from Nelson Mandela seriously: "Your playing small does not serve the world. Who are you not to be great?"

You might wonder why this book focuses on a controversial figure in history and his method for the selection of his helpers and assistants called disciples. I believe you scored him poorly for selecting the scums of the earth (so to speak) as his ambassadors. I also know that you believe you would have done better by selecting the best of the best in society including, but not limited to well-rounded and educated, learned, professional and well-loved men and women of the society as your ambassadors. Yes, I know this through the method of selection people use when recruiting their employees and making friends.

Section I
01 Introduction

Now there was also a dispute among them, as to which of them should be considered the greatest. And He said to them, "The kings of the Gentiles exercise lordship over them, and those who exercise authority over them are called 'benefactors.' But not so among you; on the contrary, he who is greatest among you, let him be as the younger, and he who governs as he who serves. For who is greater, he who sits at the table, or he who serves? Is it not he who sits at the table? Yet I am among you as the One who serves. — Luke 22:24-27 (NKJV)

Great Men Defined

Great men are people (male or female) who have been chosen before the foundation of the universe and given the mandate to serve their people, become helpers of the helpless and advocates to the marginalized minority of their society. They help pursue the freedom and emancipation of their fellow humans from their oppressors. These people are both mentally, emotionally, and spiritually matured men and women in the society, but they are exceedingly rare.

The 12 Disciples of Great men is a book written from inspiration about the life and ministry of Jesus Christ to help anyone and everyone to achieve their divine calling into greatness. It is a book that exposes the hidden secrets behind the call and commissioning of the twelve disciples of Jesus Christ. This book aspires to increase amounts of great men and women in each society, making the world a better place.

Riches and wealth do not translate to greatness in humans. **No amount of money can make a man great, the singular prerequisite to greatness is a life of service to humanity.** The service mentioned here is the service to the lowly placed in the society; people who are the minority in the society. The dominants are the oppressors in the society. There is suffering worse than death of a generation whenever there are no great men standing up for their weak. There are good deeds ordinary men have and can do that will make other people regard them as excellent individual. I have done an impressive deal of work on my other book series "Acts of Greatness" which chronicles and analyzes great deeds of ordinary and great people of the past and present.

Bob Marley understood this when he said that: "The greatness of a man is not in how much wealth he acquires, but in his integrity and his ability to affect those around him positively". **Jesus Christ called pre-ordained and ordinary men from the streets and turned them into extra-ordinary men in the Kingdom of Heaven.** By the time you complete the reading of this book and apply its secrets thereof; both in your personal, spiritual, and business lives, you will find yourself at the top of the food chain.

Jesus foresaw some special attributes and values in all his disciples that we cannot perceive in plain sight. These values include but not limited to boldness, smartness, thunder, dependability, practicality, integrity, skepticism, discipline, anonymity, zeal, patriotism, and frugality. This book will teach you how to build these values in yourself, apply them to your business ethics and use them to relate with your society. Martin Luther King Jr. realized this secret earlier while he was alive and said, "There is some good in the worst of us and some evil in the best of us. When we discover this, we are less prone to hate our enemies."

Fame is not the same as greatness, and one should not become overzealous about becoming famous. Fame comes due to diligence and favor of God in one's career, but greatness comes through service to the minorities of the society. There are so many famous people who are not great individuals. You might not be famous today, but anyone can aspire to be great any day. The 12 Disciples of Great Men will surely show you the steps to becoming a great man in a few days. Martin Luther King Jr. said, "Not everybody can be famous, but everybody can be great, because greatness is determined by service."

Human life is incomplete if it has not affected other lives positively while it lasted. Living to be 100 years or over is not worth celebrating, but it is the amount of values we have deposited in the life of other people that matter. Every human being has seeds of greatness, excellent values and talents embedded in them, which are designed to make a difference in the life of his neighbors and every other human being in his generation. I know there are many a man who have lived and died with their gifts and talents still wrapped in foil; this is the reason we have so many treasures in the graveyards.

So, I challenge you today as you read this book **to make haste and unfold the talents that are embedded in you** to serve your community because many lives depend on those talents. Nelson Mandela understood this and said, "What counts in life is not the mere fact that we have lived. It is what difference we have made to the lives of others that will determine the significance of the life we lead."

Great Men Defined

02 Choice, Selection & Election

Natural Selection Laws

"One general law, leading to the advancement of all organic beings, namely, multiply, vary, let the strongest live and the weakest die." — Charles Darwin, The Origin of Species

The renowned scientists Charles Darwin observed nature and rightly concluded that nature favors the strongest; the rich gets richer and the poor poorer. In the animal kingdom, **there is always an oppression mentality**, both animals (lower or higher) usually select the fittest in the society for any adventure by using the natural and unwritten laws of elimination of the weaker ones. In the lower animal kingdom, the fittest feed on the weakest on the food-chain.

Up in the higher animal kingdom, the fittest use the weaker ones as prey, hence the survival of the fittest. **Over time, the society automatically eliminates the weakest**, and the weaker ones become the weakest and the target for the bullying of the fittest. In this dog-eat-dog system, the fit (rich) becomes richer while the weak (poor) become poorer; so-to-speak.

Jesus Christ, who is the greatest man who lived on earth and our model for this book did not follow this **unwritten code of systemic victimization and oppression**, but surprised humanity with his divine selection formula. Jesus Christ of Nazareth is not an ordinary man. He is a supernatural being who came down to the earth as a sacrificial lamb for the salvation and restoration of the fallen man back to the kingdom of heaven. His actions were not human, and his choice of disciples was not an exception to his divine style.

Faith and Sight

For we walk by faith, not by sight. - 2 Corinthians 5:7 (NKJV)

Jesus has a divine principle behind all his actions and teachings and one of the golden rules he uses is to walk by faith and not by sight. Jesus taught the disciples to live by faith and not by sight when in John 20:29 he rebukes and corrects Thomas after his resurrection. Thomas doubted his resurrection rumors and wanted physical evidence, and Jesus finally appeared to him and showed him evidence.

Walking by sight is the normal way humans understand and operate. This means as humans we decide from what we observe, know, and understand. **Pre-knowledge and experience inform human actions**, and it is confirmed and authenticated by reasonable proofs and a body of evidence. This causes humans to apply both the written and unwritten laws of natural selection (comparison and elimination) during decision-making and conflict resolution. This method is proven to be an error, as Francesco Petrarca said, "Rarely do great beauty and great virtue dwell together." Consider both of your shopping experience and spousal selection, you will see yourself comparing items before choosing the best to buy. There are various options at the disposal of a shopper in a store; including but not limited to color, size, material, safety, sustainability, durability, and price tag, etc. The shopper goes through rigorous and strenuous process of comparing similar items from different vendors before deciding on the best.

In the case of spousal selection, one takes into consideration many key values and points including but not limited to height, body build, weight, beauty, skin tone and color, ethnicity, education, socio-economic-status, emotional and intellectual maturity, age, belief system, addiction and social life, etc. No amount of vetting and careful examination has ever prevented mistakes in human choices which usually lead to product returns and refunds, divorce, fights, and wars. It is a characteristic of sight-walking person to always miss the valuables in any choice. Humans are always pre-occupied with first impressions; and often have ended in misjudgments of character and personality. Humans judge character by whatever they can understand about the subject (person in question).

Some humans who have had ample experience in the **unwritten laws of first impressions** have won many hearts and have broken more hearts than the innocent and average Joe. The subject is systemic deception as a rule of winning; where the experienced fellow applies the laws of first impressions to confuse the subject into believing that the con man is the ideal choice because he or she acted politely and had no red flags. This pretense confuses humans because we always want the best of the best, the perfect person, and no one ever wants an average person for a companion. Considering that humans are not perfect, the less-desirables with lower socio-economic status in the society become the victims and survivors and are usually rejected in every way and situation.

The winning usually goes to the evil (presumed perfect) people in the society at the expense of the upright (presumed weak) people. The presumed perfect people of the society have done more harm to the society than the meek. We relinquish our power to the evil people in our society, by empowering them to manipulate, victimize and enslave us every time we make an uninformed choice.

We put our generations in utter darkness every time we choose by sight; the people who have mastered the unwritten laws of selection therefore have the means to apply these rules and fool us to believing in their false subtlety and civility. My summary of the imperfection in human judgment is that; **beauty is ephemeral and physical appearance is illusory, both lead to errors in judgment**. Many wars have been lost and won, many families and relationships have been destroyed by this imperfection, yet the end is not in sight. This means we all will still revel in this malady for ages to come.

Faith and Sight

Faith Redefined

> *Now faith is the substance of things hoped for, the evidence of things not seen.*
> *— Hebrews 11:1 (NKJV)*

Walking by faith is a divine and strange phenomenon. It refers to the process of judgment and decision-making not based on a body of physical proofs or evidence; but from a belief in the unknown, also on divine revelation from an unseen deity (God). It is a spiritual way of life, where physical or material evidence and occurrences are not considered in decision-making but are believed to have spiritual connotations and interpretations. It is a popular belief that the spiritual world controls the physical one. The Spiritual realm is a higher consciousness that transcends human understanding. According to Martin Luther King Jr., "Faith is taking the first step even when you can't see the whole staircase."

Divine Election by Grace

The human method of selection depends on the abilities and capabilities of the subjects involved; the fittest becomes the winner. But the heavenly method of selection is the election by grace, which does not depend on the works of the subjects involved. The Kingdom of Heaven usually selects the weakest in a subset of the people and endows them with spiritual gifting to the envy of the high and mighty.

> *Blessed be the God and Father of our Lord Jesus Christ, who has blessed us with every spiritual blessing in the heavenly places in Christ, just as He chose us in Him before the foundation of the world, that we should be holy and without blame before Him in love, having predestined us to adoption as sons by Jesus Christ to Himself, according to the good pleasure of His will, to the praise of the glory of His grace, by which He made us accepted in the Beloved. —Ephesians 1:3-6 (NKJV)*

These weaklings have been selected even before the foundations of the universe and everything thereof. Then the time comes for them to be conceived and born into the world as infants. Their survival is usually tough, but sure. They are always trained by the issues and circumstances of life which they learn to harness to their benefit. The selection of the twelve disciples was not done when Jesus called them, but they were **pre-selected before the foundations of the universe** and so is every one of us. **We have all been pre-selected to perform certain assignments on our journey through this realm back to eternity.** The selected weaklings are usually more experienced in the experiential affairs of life than the best fit ones because most of them are of humble birth and beginnings. The weaklings learn to use the same rocks thrown at them to develop their resume.

These men have been purified through the fiery furnace and have become like pure gold even in the wild. Election by grace helps maintain balance in the society where power is shared equally between the mighty and the weaklings of the society. This automatically creates natural checks and balances in a society. The mighty is humbled by this fact.

At that time Jesus said, "I praise you, Father, Lord of heaven and earth, because you have hidden these things from the wise and learned, and revealed them to little children. Yes, Father, for this is what you were pleased to do. — Matthew 11:24-26 (NIV)

By divine principle, God himself hides certain knowledge from the wise men of the world, but reveals them to unlearned men to maintain an egalitarian society. This was the case in the selection of the disciples even before the foundation of the earth. Jesus would have selected educated men, but he selected ordinary men from the society and trained them to become respected teachers and evangelists. Today their names are remembered from all over the world.

Everyone who reads the Bible calls on the names of the apostles and even the prophets of old who were chosen by God to become his spokespeople. If Jesus had chosen educated men to become his disciples, the story would have been told differently today. There would have been so much marginalization and oppression from the educated people of the society. Life would have become more unbearable for ordinary men in the society.

God Elected Pharaoh

> *So then it is not of him who wills, nor of him who runs, but of God who shows mercy. For the Scripture says to the Pharaoh, "For this very purpose I have raised you up, that I may show My power in you, and that My name may be declared in all the earth." Therefore He has mercy on whom He wills, and whom He wills He hardens. --Romans 9:16-18 (NKJV)*

There is a story in the Bible about Pharaoh, the king, and the suffering of the children of Israel in Egypt. It is a controversial story, but I want to point something out the relates to election by grace. God chose the Pharaoh to show God's mightiness to the world. God said I have raised you up, which means I formed you before the foundations of the earth and I gave you life. It depicts life after death; and death being nothingness. God's election by grace does not mean he only selects righteous people to do outstanding things all the time, but **God also selects other people to do other deeds in time.** Pharaoh was one of them. After Pharaoh, the strongman, there has been many other people in our history who are also noted for other than beneficial deeds. These people did not select themselves, but God created them to do whatever they did for his pleasure. God always has a purpose for everything that he permits on earth.

Balance in Nature

You might blame God for many things you dislike or lack understanding of, but that will change nothing, anyway. However, whatever has been written, has been written. In the universe, we need to have balance, there must be an equal occurrence of good and evil for us to achieve a balance in the universe. We should not expect to have all profitable times and no unpleasant times. **Wherever there is a positive there also will be a corresponding negative to balance the situation.**

Wherever there is a yes there will also be a no somewhere. We are stuck between night and day; while some people have a day, others might have a night. While some people sleep, some other people are awake. The entire world cannot all have the same times and seasons, we cannot all have daytime or nighttime simultaneously, there must be differences in times. This is the reason we have different time zones.

And we know that all things work together for good to those who love God, to those who are called according to His purpose. For whom He foreknew, He also predestined to be conformed to the image of His Son, that He might be the firstborn among many brethren. Moreover, whom He predestined, these He also called; whom He called, these He also justified; and whom He justified, these He also glorified. --Romans 8:28-30 (NKJV)

The 12 Disciples of Great Men focuses on the spiritual side of things and promises to expose hidden secrets to the reader regarding choices and decisions in life and business.

Jesus the Master selected 12 ordinary men as his helpers because he had a divine and revelation knowledge about all the men he called to his service that even the men did not know about themselves. Jesus is the Son of God and was present during the creation of man, so he knows every man even before inception and birth. Jesus called these men because He had created them with positive values that only He could see.

03 All Men are Created Equal but Unique

God created every man equal but unique; every man has a unique value different from another. Even a twin has unique qualities and values. Same is demonstrated in the study of our uniqueness in the area of human identity including our DNA and fingerprints; no two individuals have same of these identities. This technology has been used in the solution of crimes better than any other method. Crimes committed and covered up for ages are suddenly brought to light when there is an examination of former exhibits through use of DNA technology. This is a proof that all humans have hidden values unique to them and if harnessed, they can become the best of the best in society irrespective of their present life situations.

Every occurrence has economic importance for people who are elected by grace. These special people have to go through special seasons in their lives for them to fulfill their life's purposes and destinies. Therefore, nothing happens by chance or accident, everything has been written even before the foundations of the earth was laid. Everything happens exactly as planned by God for them to fulfill God's purpose in their lives. Then at the end of their journeys, they are received into God's glory, and they receive a crown.

But you are a chosen generation, a royal priesthood, a holy nation, His own special people, that you may proclaim the praises of Him who called you out of darkness into His marvelous light; who once were not a people but are now the people of God, who had not obtained mercy but now have obtained mercy. -- 1 Peter 2:9-10 (NKJV)

Every Man Has Treasures Embedded in Them

The fact is God has elected every living person as one of his servants. For God created us to serve him and do his will for our lives by fulfilling our life's purposes and destinies. We all have been specially crafted and endowed with special gifts and talents that we have to discover, develop, and deploy in our lives and our environments for the will of God for our lives to be fulfilled.

We all have treasures embedded in us that are not visible to the naked eyes, but we have to look inside our souls to find them. The entire universe awaits this discovery because many lives and other destinies are tied to our manifestation. All human beings created by God are like acres of diamonds waiting to be discovered.

For the earnest expectation of the creature waiteth for the manifestation of the sons of God. — Romans 8:19 (KJ21)

The principles in this book are meant for people who wish to become great men in the Kingdom of Heaven. The aspiring great man will have to apply these principles to their daily living including but not limited to vetting, selection, choice, judgment, and decision-making. These principles are available to men and women from all over the world, both in spiritual and business circles.

Mentorship vs Discipleship

"He who cannot be a good follower cannot be a good leader."— Aristotle

If you ever aspire to become a great man in life, you will have to become a disciple under someone who has significant values that you admire, and who is a great man. You need a mentor who has experience in life as a great man and who is willing to train you to become one. A disciple is an assistant or helper who is recruited by a master. The master is someone with a noble destiny and needs help in spreading his message or populating his kingdom. The Master teaches his helpers his ideology and makes them understand his purpose and destiny. The master does not merely accept everyone but selects diverse people with unique qualities into his camp.

The master in question becomes the teacher and mentor to his helpers and takes his time to train them to become independent fishers-of-men for his purpose. The master then commissions his helpers and releases them into the wild (world) to recruit more people into the master's kingdom. Then the disciples later become Apostles who are independent masters with their own disciples.

In the secular world, a disciple is either an apprentice, an employee, an associate, or a consultant recruited, trained, and deployed to help conduct business for the business owners (masters) to generate a profit. The stakes are usually high; the business owner does not merely pick anyone on the street to assume the employee position but advertises and searches for a specific set of people with certain qualifications and a wealth of experience in specific and relevant fields as employees or associates.

Virtual Discipleship

This book explores more on personal or virtual disciples (principles) of a man and a kingdom business (a business established by believers in God for the purpose of helping and not oppressing the people). Virtual disciples are certain spiritual values and morals that are needed in a man to enable him to navigate the route from an ordinary man into a great man in the kingdom of heaven. Imagine what would happen when a man cultivates these positive values from the 12 Disciples of Jesus Christ; he would become a superhuman.

The calling and utilization of the disciples made Jesus Christ the greatest man to ever walk the earth whose name is the most known globally, ages ago and even in the ages to come. **Jesus Christ started and instituted the first multi-level marketing conglomerate and franchise on earth.** He trained his core followers who in turn trained others and the never-ending chain and network goes on and on. The wisdom in this book will propel you exponentially up the food chain and above your peers and competition.

Life is All About Selling

Our daily life is all about conscious and subconscious trades; we use what we have to get what we want. **Life is also an exchange of values.** An employee sells his time and energy to a businessman in exchange for money to pay his bills. The employee does not have power over his official work hours the moment he accepts a job. He strives to satisfy his employer by doing whatever the employer demands within official work hours. It is a contract that matters to both the employer and the employee.

The employer agrees to pay the employee an extra amount of money whenever the employee spends extra time other than the stipulated time on the job as overtime pay. The employer can also refuse to pay the employee in case of unreported absence from duty. Selling is all about marketing of a product to as many prospective buyers as possible.

Fishing vs Evangelism and Marketing

In the Jesus story, he used fishing as sales and marketing. Jesus recruited more fishermen into his camp than people of other professions. He openly declared to one disciple that he wants him who was a fisher-of-fish to become a fisher-of-men in the kingdom of heaven. **Fishing here refers to the acquisition of devotees from the wild into a glorious position and better situation by offering a free service or items to the prospective devotees.** It involves the application of both words and actions that entice the subjects to agreeing with the fisher-of-men and join their kingdom. The disciples, evangelists, salesmen and marketers use this principle to gain new customers and converts. Jesus applied this principle and taught the people a new covenant which was extremely hard to understand. He was a revolutionary on earth, and he introduced another way of life which the people did not understand. The people wanted a warrior king, but Jesus taught nonviolence.

> *"Is it so bad, then, to be misunderstood? Pythagoras was misunderstood, and Socrates, and Jesus, and Luther, and Copernicus, and Galileo, and Newton, and every pure and wise spirit that ever took flesh. To be great is to be misunderstood." — Ralph Waldo Emerson.*

People never understood Jesus Christ, even when he was on earth. It was not only the society who did not understand him and his teachings, but also his disciples. They were always asking him questions because they could not understand exactly what he was talking about. His teachings were completely out of this world, and he had to take time to explain some of them to his disciples only.

The life of a great man is always filled with misunderstandings. This is because a great man does not think and act the same way the common people do, instead he invents a way of doing things uniquely.

Section Summary

1. Greatness means service to humanity
2. Anyone can attain greatness, male or female
3. Fame is not greatness
4. Wealth is not greatness
5. Human life begins before inception and birth
6. Every human has unique values, or treasures embedded in them
7. Your life is incomplete until you add positive values to other lives
8. Every human action has been pre-designed before the foundation of the universe
9. Kind people have been pre-designed to do splendid things
10. Evil people have been pre-designed to do evil deeds
11. People become outstanding by learning from outstanding people

12. The universe needs both good and evil for balance and so are great men

12 General Qualities of Greatness

"Not all of us can do great things. But we can do small things with great love."
— Mother Teresa

Greatness does not lie in great deeds, but in insignificant sacrificial deeds to put a smile on someone's face. At a glance, below, are 12 preliminary and general qualities of greatness in people and how this book can turn you from an ordinary man into a great man like Jesus Christ:

1.   Great men appreciate the best in other people. Jesus realized untapped greatness in the ordinary 12 men that human eyes could not perceive (John 1:46-51). You will learn how to hunt for positive values and attributes in people.

2.   Great men respect constituted authority and pay their taxes. Jesus himself paid taxes and asked the people to also pay their taxes (Matthew 17:24-27, Matthew 22:17-22). You will learn how to respect your government and pay your personal and business taxes whether or not you like the rulers.

3.   Great men do not judge a book by its cover. Jesus did not go in search of acceptable and educated men of the society (Matthew 9:9-13). You will learn how to look beyond the glamor in people and situations to find the essence of the matter.

4.   Great men do not support violence. Jesus taught the disciples to avoid using violence to fight oppression even by healing the ear of the arresting officer (Matthew 26:47-56). You will learn how to use prayer and other spiritual weapons for non-violent warfare.

5.   Great men walk an extra mile with other people and avoid jumping into conclusions. Jesus does not condemn sinners but gives

Section Summary

them second chances (John 8:1-11). You will learn how to forgive people and give people second chances before coming into conclusions about their personality and character instead of condemning people at first sight for their mistakes.

6. Great men give to humanity. They become advocates to the poor and fight their causes. Jesus fed the hungry, healed the sick and raised the dead (Matthew 14:13-21, John 4:46-47, Luke 7:11-18, Matthew 8:28-34, Matthew 9:18-26, John 11:1-46)). You will learn how to give to the needy in the society, especially in times of special needs.

7. Great men believe in equal opportunities in life. They believe that if given equal opportunities, all people have the inner capabilities to become one of the greatest in the society. Jesus gave equal opportunity to all the disciples, and even to Peter, who denied him, Thomas, who doubted him, and Judas Iscariot, who was to betray him (John 13:27, Matthew 26:34, John 20:24-29). You will learn how to discover talents in your society.

8. Great men believe in equality and do not discriminate against other humans based on race, sex, skin color or socio-economic status. Jesus commissioned his disciples to travel to the outermost parts of the earth and spread the gospel (Acts 1:7-8, Mark 16:15-16, Matthew 28:19-20, Luke 14:23, Mark 16:15). You will learn how to treat and accept all people equally and to live above racism and discrimination.

9. The great man is not rude; he is economical with what comes out of his mouth. Jesus had all the powers but allowed himself to be treated as someone powerless (Matt. 27:12-14). You will learn how to become respectful towards all people in all circumstances.

10. A great man controls his tongue; he does not think with his tongue or his mouth, but he considers his words before he speaks them. Jesus was careful with whatever he said to the people because he knew he was anointed, and whatever he said instantly became a spiritual law (Matthew 21:19). You will learn how to apply the 80/20 rule to control your tongue. This also applies to your interactions on social media.

11. The great man, just like any other man, is not infallible; he is capable of mistakes and emotions, but he owns up to his mistakes and makes corrections. Jesus was also human and even prayed for the cup of death to pass by him (Matthew 26:39). You will learn how to be teachable and humble. You will also learn how to accept your flaws and imperfections as a human.

12. He is not too proud to learn from every man and under any circumstance. Jesus was moved by the wisdom of the Gentile woman who proved she also needed the Savior (Matthew 15:21-28). You will learn how to make the best of every situation you face at all times without complaining.

I can go on and on about these divine qualities of great men who are everywhere, but you seldom hear their voices. These men and women are the backbones of their society and champions to the weak. They take-on the non-violent fight with the oppressors and mighty men of the society to defend the weak ones. They offer their lives for the survival of the weak ones in their society, even though they might not live long enough to reap the benefits of their labor on earth.

Section Summary

SECTION II

The 12 Disciples' Positive Values & Principles

You did not choose Me, but I chose you and appointed you that you should go and bear fruit, and that your fruit should remain, that whatever you ask the Father in My name He may give you. -- John 15:16 (NKJV)

These are the 12 principles derived from the personalities of each of the 12 disciples of Jesus Christ. They are the positive values we extract from each of the disciples. The disciples were ordinary and were not without flaws and human errors; but Jesus chose them all for their positive values. Jesus realized and can perceive positive values in everyone and give anyone the benefit of the doubt or another chance at life.

The well-rounded great man will have to apply all these principles in accurate proportions to make it to the top of the food chain. Learn to recognize the desirable values in people and overlook the negatives because we are all human and are only striving to be perfect; and one day we will attain perfection in Jesus Christ our Lord.

These values include but not limited to Boldness, Smartness, Thunder, Dependability, Practicality, Integrity, Skepticism, Discipline, Anonymity, Zeal, Patriotism and Frugality.

I have listed these values, one per chapter of this book. I believe you will find them useful and applicable to your cause. I embolden quotable quotes (strong) to stand out from the text.

Chapter 01
The Boldness of Peter

... Let us define Boldness as a conscious decision to face challenges by applying improvised methods of problem solving.

Peter (Simon Peter)

Now when the men of the Sanhedrin (Jewish High Court) saw the confidence and boldness of Peter and John, and grasped the fact that they were uneducated and untrained [ordinary] men, they were astounded, and began to recognize that they had been with Jesus. -- Acts 4:13 (AMP)

Peter was the head of the disciples because he had leadership qualities that enabled him to deal fairly with the other twelve disciples. He was a professional fisherman and was an ordinary man like the rest of the disciples. Peter's boldness came when he became the spokesperson for the twelve disciples, he was an uneducated man; but after learning at the feet of Jesus, he could stand up and preach to a crowd of people fluently and with boldness. Peter was never trained to be a public speaker, all he knew was some communication with the weather, the body of waters and fishes. After being selected and trained by Jesus, Peter became a bold public speaker in the Kingdom of Heaven. Peter could overcome his fear of public speaking after his brush with Jesus. Mandela noted, "I learned that courage was not the absence of fear, but the triumph over it. The brave man is not he who does not feel afraid, but he who conquers that fear."

Become a Voice to the Voiceless

There are so many voiceless people in the society who need your voice. They need someone to speak for them in defense against dehumanization. You got to speak up for them. Shannon L. Alder advised and said, "If you were born with the ability to change someone's perspective or emotions, never waste that gift. It is one of the most powerful gifts God can give—the ability to influence."

The aspiring great man should learn how to address a crowd confidently. In his life he would constantly have meetings with many people and some people might not be that approachable. Some audiences will be hostile and unwelcoming, so the great man should prepare and be bold enough to speak to anyone, anytime, and anywhere but with humility and without fear. The exemplary man will have some employees or associates who are high class individuals and can intimidate anyone. Some people too can play on your emotions either to get something from you or cause you to make wrong business decisions.

By becoming the voice to the voiceless, you automatically become their advocate and backbone. You receive blessings and prayers for success on your way up the ladder of life as a reward.

Take Monumental Risks

Peter the Disciple was known for taking risks, especially when he walked on water to meet the Lord Jesus. He is the only man on record who walked on water after Jesus, his master. He knew so much about water because of his profession as a fisherman. He stepped onto the water and walked towards his master, ignoring the consequences. Although he later missed it when he as human took his gaze away from Jesus and faced the storm which was coming after him as a test, but he knew his master would always save him from every danger. The great man should be ready to take risks both in his personal life and business circle. **When one knows the risk involved in any endeavor but still goes ahead with the plan, he is practicing boldness.** Every decision we make has high levels of risk, the higher the risk, the higher the benefits in any situation. The businessman would have to take substantial risks to realize enormous profits. He should be ready to face failure, boldly, and without regret. No business opportunity is worth taking if it does not have higher levels of risk because they might not be profitable enough or worth the while.

Learn How to Deal with Failure

"Only those who dare to fail greatly can ever achieve greatly." — Robert F. Kennedy

A great man learns how to deal with constructive failures and turns them into outstanding successes in his life. **Constructive failure in this book refers to those minor setbacks and negative outcomes in a project or dashes in hope.** The great man should be ready to face constructive failures arising from his decisions in life and business, because these are inevitable. **Constructive failures are steps in the ladder of success**; without constructive failures, there would be no success in business and life situations. Constructive failures are not fatal but should be considered positive steps to success as it eliminates the wrong options in the list of many options on the table.

Negative results are not failures and should not be treated as one, rather we should treat them as minor successes. Destructive failure happens when a man gives up every hope, stops attempting, and then dies in the state of despair. **Destructive failure is only determined at the point of death** because as long as a man lives and breathes, he can always turn things around for himself and his generation, but as soon as he dies, everything ends right there. **Therefore, you are not a failure as long as you can breathe**, God gives everyone fresh chances and opportunities to achieve whatever they want in life. Robert T. Kiyosaki explains and said, "In school we learn that mistakes are bad, and we are punished for making them. Yet, if you look at the way humans are designed to learn, we learn by making mistakes. We learn to walk by falling down. If we never fell down, we would never walk."

Stop Complaining and Murmuring

The man who aspires to become a great man should not become a complainer or murmurer. **Excessive complaints are traits of people who would not go far in life** because they never realize opportunities around them, and they become bitter and envious when they see other people progressing around them. They always look for mistakes in other people to complain about, even when it has nothing to do with them. They apply the unwritten laws of destructive criticism to bring down every person they come across. They always have something bad to say about anybody, and they form groups of gossipers. **Therefore, anyone who wants to be great in life should not become a friend of complainers**. They should not also indulge in bringing other people down even when those people deserve to be, but always find a way to say good things about people and give second chances. Maya Angelou rightly advises and said, "What you're supposed to do when you don't like a thing is change it. If you can't change it, change the way you think about it. Don't complain."

Forgive the Past and Move-On

'Unforgiveness' is the refusal to let go of past wrongs. Great men forgive the wrongdoings of the past and focus on the present. **Unforgiveness is the worst burden and self-inflicted slavery that exists across the board**. This completely blocks all forms of progress of an individual. It is even dangerous to our health because it affects the normal workings of the heart. **Unforgiveness kills more than cancer** and not merely physical death but emotional death, which turns a man into a zombie or living death even while still breathing. This makes progress impossible and every man who wants to become a great man must forgive and forget the past for him to have today and tomorrow. It does not matter what the offense was, the more you hold onto it, the more it forces you to remain at that spot for the rest of your life. Martin Luther King Jr. rightly said, "I have decided to stick to love...Hate is too great a burden to bear."

Improvise, Improvise, Improvise

"It is what we make out of what we have, not what we are given, that separates one person from another." — Nelson Mandela

Boldness is also expressed when the man acts innovatively in the face of difficulties and confusion. Times and Seasons would certainly come when the man will be pushed to the wall or meet a brick wall with no options on the table. At this juncture, he will have to think innovatively by exploring fresh ideas and solutions for the situation. You should not give up when you're not presented with options in a tight situation, but always look inwards into your heart and soul and think about a distinct way of solving the problem, because every problem has a solution. It is only tough people who meet tough situations and face it squarely. Weak-minded people shy away from tough situations, and weak-minded people never become outstanding people.

Invent New Products, Ideas and Solutions

Great men always search for and find new ways and technologies for achieving success. Every time you see new products in the market you should understand a great man somewhere has been applying his time and energy to research and has finally brought those products to life from his innovative faculty. **There are billions of novel ideas that are waiting to be discovered** by men and you might just be the one who has the divine unction to invent some splendid stuff. If you are still sleeping, I bid you wake up and look inside of you and find that product or products and ideas for the universe and this whole generation of people are waiting for such products. Human beings invented the computers, cell phone technologies, telecommunications, the Internet, robots, medicine, and many other solutions to man's prevalent problems, and you might have something in you that your generation needs urgently.

Abandon Distractions

Abandon whatever is standing on your way to your destiny. Nothing else matters in life but your life's purpose and destiny. Peter took a risk by abandoning his fishing business to follow Jesus (who was his destiny) even without question. That was a serious decision on Peter's part. This is a proof Peter was created for this day, that he would be called upon by the spirit in him to answer to the call of his creator. Jesus' communication with Peter was not physical but spiritual. Jesus spoke to Peter's spirit, and Peter also responded in the spirit. That was why he physically said nothing because he literally had nothing to say.

I believe Peter's spirit was rejoicing and saying something like 'Yes, this is the day that the Lord has made, I will rejoice and be glad in it.' The ordinary man Peter did not know exactly what he was doing, but his spirit man knew exactly what he was doing. He abandoned everything by the sea and followed Jesus, not minding his survival. And today we can read about the acts of Peter the Apostle. Are you ready to die for something today to realize your destiny as Martin Luther King Jr. said: "A man who won't die for something is not fit to live?" Every man who aspires to become a great man should be ready to abandon or sacrifice so much in pursuit of spiritual manifestation. **Nothing should be too much for you to abandon in pursuit of your purpose and destiny, nothing.** Your divine purpose should become your number one goal in life, and you have to pursue it with everything you have got. **Nothing should be of more importance than the manifestation of the gifts of God in you.**

Friends, family, and other material things in the world should never stand in your way of progress. Your enemy knows your purpose and destiny, so he constantly tries to put obstacles in your way, to prevent you from progressing. The enemy has a formula which is to confuse you into thinking that other concerns are more important in your life than your life's purpose and destiny, but he is always a liar and will remain a liar for ages to come.

Sacrifice Your Wealth

Jesus said to him, "If you want to be perfect, go, sell what you have and give to the poor, and you will have treasure in heaven; and come, follow Me." But when the young man heard that saying, he went away sorrowful, for he had great possessions. -Matthew 19:21-22 (NKJV)

Money when given much power can cause a man to misbehave in life and so might not fulfill his life's purpose and destiny. The actual principle about money that every man should know is **money is not meant to be stored up, but it is meant to be given out freely** and to whoever needs help, for this is the only way of storing wealth in the bank of heaven.

Cast your bread upon the waters, for you will find it after many days. Give a serving to seven, and also to eight, for you do not know what evil will be on the earth. — Ecclesiastes 11:1-2 (NKJV)

Casting your bread upon the waters refers to the act of giving your money to support the poor in the society. This is the major way of giving money to God or offering your wealth to God. **Every man who wants financial blessings should learn how to give to the poor**, for it is another way of lending to God and investing your money in the bank of heaven. This involves giving sacrificially and expecting nothing back. This is another risk that speeds up a man on the ladder of success and greatness in the Kingdom of Heaven.

Consider the great men of old who became philanthropists and are well-known for giving to the poor in times of critical need. According to Mother Teresa, "At the end of life we will not be judged by how many diplomas we have received, how much money we have made, how many great things we have done. We will be judged by "I was hungry, and you gave me something to eat, I was naked, and you clothed me. I was homeless, and you took me in."

To progress in life, the man who is aspiring to become a great man should sit down and count his valuables, especially those matters he believes he can never let go off. He should then attempt to detach himself from those valuables because they might simply be blocking his progress to greatness. The man should also list all his habits and find the ones that seem so difficult to let go of.

There are some habits we know are deterrents to our progress, but sometimes we are so attached to them we might live with them and rather trash our life, purpose, and destiny. This is not meant to happen because it would have cost our divine calling and whoever is not yielding fruits will surely be cut down and thrown into the fire.

Sacrifice Your Time

Another risk worth taking as a requirement to become a great man is sacrificing one's valuable time to support people in the society. Time is money and your time means much money to you but if you should become a great man in life, you will have to learn how to sacrifice some of your valuable time to help other people in the society and community. It is about getting involved in community service and volunteerism which does not generate a profit to you but directly benefits the society positively.

This is often more valuable to the community than merely offering financial support. Nelson Mandela said, "During my lifetime I have dedicated myself to this struggle of the African people. I have fought against white domination, and I have fought against black domination. I have cherished the ideal of a democratic and free society in which all persons live together in harmony and with equal opportunities. It is an ideal which I hope to live for and to achieve. But if needs be, it is an ideal for which I am prepared to die."

I assume you have an idea to start a non-profit; I encourage you to revive your interest and go all out, people need your services.

Solve Problems Around You

The great man invokes his innovative faculty to explore the many problems in his society and then find solutions to the problems. He then turns those solutions into profitable businesses. The great man does not copy other people's businesses, but he begins his businesses from the scratch by leveraging on the problems in his society and providing solutions to them. **The great man does not go into business for the sole reason of making money**, but for the sole purpose of providing solutions to problems in his society. And money will always come back as a secondary benefit for him after his society is satisfied with his solutions.

One way to identify a great man who has explored his innovative and creative spirit is that; they always incorporate a handful of related businesses simultaneously and do not depend on other businesses to complete their goal. Their new businesses might include research, development, production, storage, distribution, training, marketing, and logistics simultaneously. They always develop a piece of their software or solution for the public to use for free as this attracts the public to their paid or premium products and services. This method makes the businessman resilient and helps him survive the competition because he does not depend on other businesses for his growth and can never be held down to ransom by anybody. Consider Google and their Gmail, Google search engine, Android system etc. which are offered for free to the public attract so much business to them. Facebook is free to the public too, and both businesses amass so much wealth globally.

Be as Bold as a Lion

The wicked flee when no one pursues, but the righteous are bold as a lion. — Proverbs 28:1 (NKJV)

The Lion is the self-acclaimed king of the forest and seems to have no contenders. The lion fears no other animal in the forest, irrespective of the size, number, and strength. They are not intimidated by the courage of other animals, but they develop a formula that gives them the wisdom to overpower any powerful animal in the forest. Deep in the dry savanna lands of the southern Africa, I watched as lions attack a herd of buffaloes and after much fight killed some of them for food. The lions have much patience as a virtue which enables them to stalk powerful animals for miles until they find a weakness in their defense. They then launch on the unsuspecting member of the herd who strays away from the entire herd and after much fight, the bull is taken down. If the lions cannot wrestle the bull down, they do not give up but keep stalking the herd of buffaloes until they succeed.

Great men take on tough tasks, especially the ones that are rejected by mere men or are regarded as impossible. They face challenges head-to-head and do not give in to fear. When noble men meet a mountain on their path, they do not despair, but they either find a way around the mountain or try to climb over it. If all else fails, then they dig a tunnel under it or blow it up. Great men do not waste too much energy in solving problems like killing a fly with an atomic bomb; they know when to use simple problem-solving methods and progress to the highest methods of response depending on the situation. Great men of the past devised a means of building railroads across mountains and rivers using this formula.

Be Persistent

Great men adopt persistence by adopting The Water Winning Formula (one of my books) in problem solving. The water we know is a universal solvent; it always tries to attack whatever stands on its way by dissolving such an obstacle if it cannot be pushed over.

"Dripping water hollows out stone, not through force but through persistence."
— *Ovid*

Water uses persistence as a winning formula, and every great man needs to learn how to be persistent in pursuit of their valuable cause, purpose, and destiny. It is true that water always finds its way. Water never gives up, even when it does not produce any sound or appear calm. **Water is a silent warrior.** Think about the water you have in a cup or any container, if you leave it for a prolonged period, water will attack the cup or container by attempting to dissolve wherever it can touch. You notice wherever the water touched becomes slippery and over time changes color. It means the water is eating into the cup or the container. When there is flash flooding, the flood water flows down the slope and keeps going until it gets to a location that prevents it from passing. It might stop there for a while and try to fill up the spot and when the spot is filled up the water overflows and keeps moving down the slope. If the spot is not strong, the water will dissolve its walls, causing the spot to either crack or break down completely and set the water free.

This means that water cannot be caged for too long, it would always break free. This same principle applies to great men. Great men are not always held captive by any knowledge forever, they always have a way of manufacturing solutions and breaking free from captivity. Great men are never idle, but every time you see them appear idle, they are always busy in their minds and deep in their thoughts. They might appear quiet but **do not mistake their quietness for idleness or naivety**.

"Great things happen to those who don't stop believing, trying, learning, and being grateful." — Roy T. Bennett

Persistence involves the act of trying again and again on any adventure without giving up. Selective persistence is the act of undertaking tough situations over time and in bits. It involves attempting tasks periodically and if one does not get desired results; they put a pause on the project and get back to it after a period.

Great men do not completely hand-off any projects that they cannot accomplish today but keep it aside and handle other matters and then get back to it in the future. And by then they must have gotten recent knowledge and wisdom on how to tackle the problem.

Chapter Summary

1. Great men do not entertain fear for the unknown
2. They become a voice to the voiceless in the society
3. They are not afraid of taking substantial risks
4. They are not afraid of minor failures
5. They do not live with the burden of unforgiveness
6. They do not depend wholly on the wisdom of others but improvise
7. They sacrifice so much in their lives to pursue their destinies
8. They are troubleshooters and problem solvers
9. They are persistent on a noble course
10. They take on matters boldly without fear or favor
11. They do not complain
12. They never give up

Chapter 02
The Smartness of Andrew

... Let us define Smartness as the ability to apply divine wisdom in problem solving.

Andrew (Peter's brother)

One of the two who heard what John said and [as a result] followed Jesus was Andrew, Simon Peter's brother. He first looked for and found his own brother Simon and told him, "We have found the Messiah" (which translated means the Christ). Andrew brought Simon to Jesus. Jesus looked at him and said, "You are Simon the son of John. You shall be called Cephas (which is translated Peter)." - John 1:40-42 (AMP)

Andrew the Disciple made a smart decision to leave John the Baptist and immediately for Jesus Christ; because John the Baptist promoted Jesus Christ as the Messiah who they were waiting for. This was a smart decision, and it did not end there. He invited his brother Peter to Jesus too. John the Baptist's ministry was to be a forerunner for Jesus Christ. He announced Jesus Christ to the people even before Jesus showed up. Andrew took the chance and opportunity to finally follow Jesus Christ. He never waited for weeks or lengthy periods of time for him to decide because he never wanted to miss the opportunity to meet the Messiah. In other words, Andrew applied divine wisdom in his choice to follow Jesus.

You Should Always Be Alert

The great man must be intelligent enough to realize every passing opportunity around him. He should open wide his entrepreneurial antenna to catch any favorable frequency that has a profitable opportunity in it. This involves the man going out and getting involved in community events and meeting people on the regular basis. The more the people you meet, the more chance you have to get to know the problems they have and the higher the probability for you to find a problem that is so serious and needs urgent solutions that you can leverage on.

The more you interact with people, the better the chance of meeting geniuses along the way who can work with you for the progress of your business. The keyword here is becoming smart and alert; being able to make quick and intelligent decisions in any situation. There are certain opportunities that might present itself to so many people in time, but whoever would act on it, ASAP takes all the glory.

Avoid Procrastination

"You cannot escape the responsibility of tomorrow by evading it today." — Abraham Lincoln

Procrastination refers to the action of delaying or postponing something. Smart people do not procrastinate, they take adequate action and make the most of the opportunity that they meet. **Procrastination is one reason people lose out in life**. The major reason for procrastination is indecision, ignorance, and fear; mostly fear of the unknown. If you wait too long to decide on such opportunities, you might lose much treasure because someone else must have already acted on it and developed a product from it. By the time you see similar ideas on TV, it would have been too late. Many people have lost their treasures this way, and they blame themselves or someone else for it.

The only time and reason you should procrastinate on matters is when it sounds too good to be true or fishy. Some new business ventures might sound too promising and get-rich-quick game, but beware, read between the lines and confirm every fact before you say yes. We can harness procrastination for the benefit of the great man in areas of avoiding illegal deals a scam.

Avoid Illegal Deals

The aspiring great man should avoid every solution or business idea that appears illegal and might become a danger to the society in the long run. Do not listen to any advice or counsel that would encourage you to go into such businesses because sooner or later your nemesis might catch up with you. Although some of those tempting opportunities are always lucrative but do not be deceived, whatever money you make out of such could not repair the damages it will bring to you and your business and even to the community at large.

Sometimes other businesses would want to do business with your business; but never be fooled, always remember to scrutinize every of their ideas and plans to make sure you understand what you would get into. Use your intelligence to view or paint a mental picture of both the new business and their ideas past, present and future. Then use your smartness to make a quick decision and, if you are not comfortable with the numbers and results, simply say no. Never consider the profit projection before considering the legality, morality, sustainability, and safety of any business venture. **It is too disastrous to consider the financial projections of a proposal before its legality and sustainability**.

Study and Learn Daily

"Live as if you were to die tomorrow. Learn as if you were to live forever." — Mahatma Gandhi

Great men listen to and decipher hidden warnings and signs from unethical and unusual sources like children, nature, and innocent people. The keyword here is to underrate nobody or any situation; brace yourself to learn from everybody every time. Some situations might appear pointless, but if you look hard enough and listen closely you would learn so many things from those situations and anybody anytime. Gold exists in the natural earth and it is mixed with clay, **one must look beyond the clay to find the gold**. If you do not take adequate time to examine the clay, you can never find the gold. Our treasures are hidden from plain sight, but if you study hard and listen long enough, you will discover so much hidden and precious gems. This is where smartness comes into play as opposed to hard work. Give an audience to everyone to speak more, while you listen more and speak less, for it is in listening that you learn everything you need from every situation and from anyone. Smartness bids you listen more and talk less by applying the 80/20 rule. **Listen 80% of the time and talk 20% of the time;** this way you will have enough time to enjoy your audience, whoever it might be.

As a great man you should not become like the elderly monkey in myths who could not be taught new tricks. It is assumed that aged monkeys have known all the tricks about how to maneuver and survive in the forest, and there is nothing new that one can teach them. Do not become like the dinosaurs that have become extinct, get yourself an education; formal or informal, and make sure you learn new concepts daily. **Behind every great man are his books**, and the authors of those books are indirectly his mentors, you have to be careful of what you read and the authors you read from.

This world is a beautiful place for men and women who take their time to learn about life and living. Conversely, life is worse than hell for people who do not have a habit of studying. When you stop learning new things, you automatically stop living. **Learning is the reason we live day by day.** Learning is the conscious effort to discover something substantial and new either by reading a book or searching the internet, etc. This includes, but not limited to fact finding, learning new trade and business opportunities, learning about other talented and successful men in your society, or trying to find the reason behind anything that bothers you. If you ever find yourself in a monotonous routine for most part of your life, it is a proof you are not learning and that you might not become a great man in life. If you keep doing the same things the same way for many years, the fact is you are like a living dead. Learning helps you do the same things you have been doing in life, but in different and better ways. A proof of smartness is the ability to do the same things in life, but in a different and better way.

Avoid Ignorance

"Nothing in the world is more dangerous than sincere ignorance and conscientious stupidity." — Martin Luther King Jr.

Ignorance is awfully expensive while smartness is ridiculously cheap. Smartness as one keyword to becoming a great man is an essential tool. You should learn fast and vastly because time does not wait for no one. The world favors men who devote their precious time to personal study and development.

Greatness Is Not Taught in College

Colleges and universities would not teach you everything you need to become a great man, because the curriculum has not been developed for that to happen, but it is left for you to develop yourself. The college will only point you to the path of life and give you basic introductions into the general principles of life, but the rest is left for you to discover, develop, and deploy. Martin Luther King Jr. said it all when he said, *"Everybody can be great...because anybody can serve. You do not have to have a college degree to serve. You do not have to make your subject and verb agree to serve. You only need a heart full of grace. A soul generated by love."* **They do not teach success and greatness in college**. Many men have become successful who have not been to or completed college and many men have failed in life who have completed college. **If you must go to college, be careful what you read because it might**

derail your purpose and vision causing you a setback and obvious delay to your destiny.

College is not for men who have not realized their life's purposes; but it is for people who have. For those who have realized their life's purposes, they will do well in college and come out to be successful in life. But for those who have not, they will only become the more confused in life. They might end up completing college but not using whatever they learned, or they might keep changing carriers and courses and end up miserable as disgruntled employees and servants to others.

Drop Out If College Interferes

"I have never let my schooling interfere with my education." — Mark Twain

There is a problem I discovered in the society, the parents dictating to their kids what to study and what schools to attend based on their own personal preferences in life. Some parents force their kids into professional careers like medicine, science, technology, law, and many more to make them fit into the elite group of the society even without the opinions of their kids. At the end, the child struggles in college, and eventually they give up and either change course or drop out.

There is another set of great men who started college but dropped out to focus on their dreams and destinies. These are men who have discovered their life's purposes and found that college and college work was interfering with their imagination and intuition. They discovered both could not mingle together and finally broke away to focus on their life's purpose and destiny rather than live on the dictates of their professors and scholars.

These exceptional men break away from college to develop their dreams and to the amazement of everyone, they succeed in life and come up with outstanding business ideas proven to be commercial and worth investing in. This attracts the attention of investors who support the idea and finance them.

> *"The only thing that interferes with my learning is my education." — Albert Einstein.*

Most of these businesses have grown to become multinational conglomerates, creating more jobs, and hiring thousands upon thousands globally. These men become employers of labor to educated people, seasoned scholars, and professors alike, which makes them masters even to the educated people who could not discover and develop their creative talents on time. The fact is everyone has a measure of gold and treasure inside him or her; and if they can discover and develop those talents on time, they suddenly become successful business leaders in their society.

You have to be smart enough to discover where you are and where you belong in the ladder of creativity and intuition to figure out whether or not to go to college. **There is no rule in the game, you must set your own rules.** There is no proof that going or not going to college would make you successful or superior in life.

Discover Your Talents Early

> *"Hide not your talents, they for use were made, What's a sundial in the shade?" — Benjamin Franklin*

Everyone is created to become successful in life with a measure of talent. Some people are created to become masters and leaders, while others are created to become followers and servants. Everyone must be clever enough to discover who they have been created to be, a leader or follower. Everyone cannot become leaders, and everyone cannot become followers simultaneously, there will always be leaders, and wherever there are leaders there will always be followers. There are more followers than leaders in the world as a single leader leads a multitude of followers in whatever way he wants. **It is now your choice to either remain a follower for life or upgrade to become a leader and a master in your generation.** The steps in this book will help you become a master and a great man in your generation.

Grab New Opportunities like Jeff Bezos

After the introduction of the internet and the world wide web, many entrepreneurs were yet to grasp its benefits to business. Jeff Bezos was among the first to discover the hidden benefits of the internet, and he could apply it to his new business idea in e-commerce. Jeff Bezos picked the books as his first merchandise to sell on the Internet. He studied and understood the speed at which the Internet was growing. He realized that thousands of people were surfing or browsing the Internet daily, and he figured it would be beneficial to sell something on the Internet to reach so many people simultaneously as opposed to a brick and mortar store. This shows a proof of smartness in business start-up ideas. Jeff Bezos sold books online not because he loved books that much, but because he studied the book category and found there were so many items in the book's category. Brick-and-mortar bookshops do not have all in-print books all in stock at any physical location or store due to space, so his idea was to build an online store that would have millions or billions of books on the same website so customers could buy any books they want anytime or any-day. Jeff recognized the new opportunity and grasped it like Andrew left John the Baptist for Jesus. So in 1995 Amazon.com was launched from his garage and as at today in 2020 Amazon.com is the most valuable company globally.

Offer Free Services Like Facebook & Google

Mark Zuckerberg (Facebook) and Larry Page (Google) to mention but a few, have something common in their lives and business. These people understand what it is to offer free services to the public, either as a form of business tactics or only plain service. They have become great men in the history of business by rising so swiftly and building multinational businesses by simply using the free services model of business. Mark Zuckerberg started Facebook and offered it to the public for free beginning with his college colleagues. He built many personal apps for his use before he built Facebook for other people to become users. This I should say has accidentally catapulted him into the upper echelon of prominent businessmen in the society. He was smart enough to grasp the opportunity in the thousands of new users of the Facebook platform and monetized that to his benefit. Today Mark is also mentioned among the top 10 richest men in the society. There are so many long-standing businesses who have produced no billionaires to date. Mark was 19, and he started something new in his dorm room, and in the face of Friendster and Myspace social networking platforms he birthed Facebook that has become a multinational business.

Larry Page and Sergey Brin built Google and offered it to the public for free. Google has now become the god of the internet; it is the best search engine out there and many businesses sworn by Google for sustenance. They also offer Gmail, which has become the greatest free online email application. And among other things they now offer the Android operating system for touchscreen mobile devices and computers. Android cellphones are used worldwide, and anyone can build devices to use the android as the operating system, all for free.

These free services act as a magnet to draw thousands and thousands of users globally to the business and statistics show the more users you have, the more profit you can make. **Now, the prevalent business model for free service platforms is to monetize the traffic with commercials and ads.** The new free service business need not sell anything to their users, but only provide a free platform for users to socialize globally. Think of a social service you can provide to people and visualize what it might turn out to be.

Offer Free Services Like Facebook & Google

Chapter Summary

1. Outstanding people learn something new daily
2. They read books
3. They watch documentaries
4. They discover their talents early in life
5. They are ingenious
6. They do not procrastinate in delicate matters
7. They catch every suitable opportunity
8. They talk less
9. They listen more
10. They stay relevant in their studies
11. They see the big picture
12. They become entrepreneurs

Chapter 03
The Thunder of James

... Let us define Thunder as the highest measure of anger that stimulates destructive action and reaction in humans. We can use it in both corrective and destructive situations.

James (son of Zebedee) the elder

James the son of Zebedee, and John the brother of James; and them he surnamed Boanerges, which is, Sons of thunder... Mark 3:17 (ASV)

Now when the time was approaching for Him to be taken up [to heaven], He was determined to go to Jerusalem [to fulfill His purpose]. He sent messengers on ahead of Him, and they went into a Samaritan village to make arrangements for Him; but the people would not welcome Him, because He was traveling toward Jerusalem. When His disciples James and John saw this, they said, "Lord, do You want us to command fire to come down from heaven and destroy them?" But He turned and rebuked them [and He said, "You do not know what kind of spirit you are; for the Son of Man did not come to destroy men's lives, but to save them."] And they journeyed on to another village. - Luke 9:51-56 (AMP)

Jesus renamed two of his disciples and called them the sons of thunder. Jesus knows what everyone is capable of doing even more than we know of ourselves. **Our true color is always shown in times of distress**, and those disciples asked for permission to call down thunder to destroy the people who resisted them. **Anger brings out our true colors.**

Publicly Denounce and Criticize Immorality

The aspiring great man should understand everyone has a measure of anger in them. Anger can be harnessed and managed only by people who are humble. Anger comes out when other people treat us badly, and we all have to be careful that we do not respond or act while we are boiling from the inside. **Anger management is key to the maturity of the aspiring great man.** Aristotle pointed out and said, "Anybody can become angry, that is easy, but to be angry with the right person and to the right degree and at the right time and for the right purpose, and in the right way, that is not within everybody's power and is not easy." Great men learn how to harness their anger for appropriate use whenever the opportunity presents itself. The two major seasons when the great man should use his thunder are to publicly declare unprofessional behavior and idea to be wrong or evil by denouncing it and show the faults of someone or something in a disapproving way by criticizing it. **The great man should not keep silent in such situations, because if no one speaks publicly against a crime or immoral act; they are indirectly endorsing such behavior as a new normal and perfect.**

The great man should develop the ability to exercise his thunder to say NO to social ills that plague our societies including but not limited to: peer pressure, bad habits, drug abuse, juvenile delinquency, theft, prostitution, thuggery, corruption, human trafficking, child poverty, child labor, child abuse, domestic violence, exploitation, racism and racial discrimination, war crimes, weapons of mass destruction, etc. The aspiring great man should never indulge in any business with people who promote these vices (immorality, wrongdoing, wickedness, evil, corruption, misconduct, ungodliness, godlessness, unholiness, unrighteousness, profanity, depravity, degeneracy, perversion, lewdness, crime, etc.)

Promote Nonviolence

And suddenly, one of those who were with Jesus stretched out his hand and drew his sword, struck the servant of the high priest, and cut off his ear. But Jesus said to him, "Put your sword in its place, for all who take the sword, will perish by the sword. Or do you think that I cannot now pray to My Father, and He will provide Me with more than twelve legions of angels? How then could the Scriptures be fulfilled, that it must happen thus?" ... Matthew 26:51-54 (NKJV)

Anger has many merits and demerits. It can make or mar one's purpose and destiny. Our Master Jesus encountered many situations that tested his ability to control his anger. Several times the people tried to arrest him, but he would not put up a fight but simply disappear. That did not make him weak or foolish. He rather used wisdom above anger to make sure he does not support any act of violence against anyone, even the oppressor.

Although the Jewish people were expecting a combatant Messiah, Jesus was wise enough not to fall into their temptation. He had to teach them that violence is not the best way for a revolution. He had to prove to them that nonviolence is the new normal. He proved this physically while the men arrested him at the garden when Peter tried to defend him with a sword by cutting off the ear of one officer, Jesus immediately rebuked Peter and fixed back the ear. This was Jesus' way of proving to the disciples that his mission was not to fight physical wars but spiritual.

In recent times there was Mahatma Gandhi, who popularized the theory of non-violence as a tool for resistance to the British colonization in India, thereby leading to their independence. He has become the originator of the non-violence method in the modern world and the entire world credits him as the most popular non-violent activist in the world. Then there was Martin Luther King Jr., a preacher and activist who led the fight for the abolition of racial discrimination in the United States of America. These men publicly condemned violence and **adopted nonviolence as their formula for solving the issues of the society**. They could control their anger and turn it to persistence without violence, and they all succeeded in the motives.

Allow Due Process

Jesus knew when to surrender to due process. He knew it was time to end his earthly ministry and conclude the work of salvation by giving-in to death on the cross. He took his inner disciples into the garden to pray and see if he could overturn his destiny on earth. This decision was one of the reasons Peter and the other disciples denied Jesus. They were all confused, and I suppose they felt some anger in them because Jesus was about to be killed, their master was about to be taken away from them.

He went a little farther and fell on His face, and prayed, saying, "O My Father, if it is possible, let this cup pass from Me; nevertheless, not as I will, but as You will." Matthew 26:39 (NKJV)

The disciples knew that Jesus had the power, but he bluntly refused to fight back. He could do miracles upon miracles and even walk on water, so he had the power to do anything he wanted to do and defend himself. Jesus chose not to take any action because it was his time to pay the ultimate price. Judas however must have considered Jesus would always defend himself, so he gambled and took the money from the terrible people. He was also disappointed, Jesus refused to fight back, and he later regretted his decision and game. Judas and the other apostles; like a baby that trusts when the father throws her up that he would always catch her, hoped that Jesus would defend himself either by fighting back or calling on the Angels to come down and kill the soldiers, but they were all disappointed. It was not until after the resurrection that they all remembered what Jesus said to them about his death and resurrection. After the resurrection, the disciples' hopes were restored, and they became bold enough to go out and preach the gospel.

"Pain and suffering are always inevitable for a large intelligence and a deep heart. The great men must, I think, have great sadness on earth." — Fyodor Dostoyevsky

I want you to take some time out and ponder about the circumstances that surrounded Jesus Christ; think of what you would have done when the officers came to arrest Jesus. The keyword here is for you to always remember **you have so much power within you**; and that you do not have to abuse your power. Sometimes you need to allow yourself to go through due process, which is inevitable in the life of great people. You must not fight everything that comes your way because great men do not always fight. Sometimes you need to allow nature to work on you, as it will make you become as refined as pure gold. We all need to pass through the refiner's fire for us to become the gold that we need to be. The beautiful plate, cup, or pot you have in your house is so beautiful to behold, but that is not possible without so much fire. These materials come in a raw form taken out from the earth and passed through fire. The raw material is burned and manipulated through the fire until every garbage is burnt out. The proper material then shows up pure and beautiful, then it is molded into whatever the potter wants.

Unleash Prayer as Your Spiritual Weapon

He answered, "Because of your little faith [your lack of trust and confidence in the power of God]; for I assure you and most solemnly say to you, if you have [living] faith the size of a mustard seed, you will say to this mountain, 'Move from here to there,' and [if it is God's will] it will move; and nothing will be impossible for you. — Matthew 17:20 (AMP)

Every believer is endowed with spiritual weapons of warfare. These are prayer points and decrees a believer uses when praying for a change in the society or when asking God for intervention in crisis. **Prayer is the key Christian method of nonviolence.** Every believer is also filled with the holy ghost and power who helps them to pray according to the will of God. The true great men should always allow the Holy Spirit to direct their thoughts and prayers and desist from taking vengeance against evil doers and oppressors. Great men surrender everything to their God in prayer and wait for His response and guidance. God himself wants his children to surrender all vengeance to him who has all the powers and the hearts of kings and strong men in his hands. Although we are equipped with these supernatural powers, we must never abuse it by using it to kill other people, even the evil men and oppressors. We should always allow the will of God be done. The great men should forgive the oppressors and hand them over to God. We should pray for God to touch their hearts and cause them to repent because God is not interested in killing evil people, but he wants all people to repent of their evil ways and turn back to God the father.

Chapter Summary

1. Great men know how to manage their anger
2. Vengeance does not consume them
3. They do not act while angry
4. They avoid violence for any reason
5. They allow vengeance to God
6. They trust in prayer as the master key
7. They only fight spiritual warfare
8. They are gentle
9. They know when to say NO
10. They are not easily angered
11. They know when to surrender to due process
12. Great men are no cowards

Chapter 04
The Dependability of John

... Let us define dependability as the gift of being reliable indeed, especially in tough times.

John (James' brother)

So Jesus, seeing His mother, and the disciple whom He loved (esteemed) standing near, said to His mother, "[Dear] woman, look, [here is] your son!" Then He said to the disciple (John), "Look! [here is] your mother [protect and provide for her]!" From that hour the disciple took her into his own home....
John 19:26-27 (AMP)

Jesus had twelve disciples, but three out of the twelve were closest to him. The three were in the inner circle as Jesus spent more time with them and took them with him to some special assignments that the others were not privy to. The three we understand were more trustworthy and reliable to his cause.

No man can be called a great man if people cannot rely on or trust him. A man's character (his mental and moral qualities) includes trustworthiness and dependability, which are the fundamental qualities that sustain him on top of the food chain longer than the rest of the competition. **People should be able to rely on you** and trust that you will always be there for them in times of need. They should be able to commit their hearts to you and go to sleep, trusting they will see you when they wake up.

Learn to Be Reliable

The society should perceive you as someone who does not falter or disappoint people. **Great men are always considered people with significant charisma**. They attract people to themselves and inspire devotion in other people, thereby creating a sense of dependability and reliability.

A man who lacks reliability is utterly useless. -Confucius

The aspiring great man should learn how not to let his people down, because these people have become their followers and fan base. They are the ones who continually sound the trumpets of the great man and announce them and their products to friends and family.

The aspiring great man should avoid any public scandal which would sabotage the relationship he has with the community, instead he should always reach out to them regularly and organize get-together, dinners, or social events to connect with his fan base.

Keep All Secrets Secret

Another way of earning the trust of your society is to learn how to keep their secrets. No one would want to get too close to you if they found out that you publicly disclosed their secrets to anyone or everyone at will. The great man should learn how to be a man of his own words by keeping every promise he has made to everyone in the past and never backing down on any outstanding matters he supported. He should not be a man who would always change his mind now and then.

Accept Civic Responsibilities

Great men are men of integrity and are always called upon to become custodians of public or group vitals. Jesus handed over his mother to the custody of John, trusting she will never be abused or molested. It is exceedingly difficult to trust anyone with another individual's affairs in this age of rape and abuse. Everyone is now becoming the victim of abuse, including boys, girls, and women. **Some evil men have become so depraved as to indulge in such acts of evil, sexual molestation and trafficking.**

> *"Ask not what your country can do for you; ask what you can do for your country." — John F. Kennedy*

It is not normal and accurate for individuals to demand their country to do anything for them when they themselves refuse to get involved in the running of the affairs of their country. Just like Kennedy said, you should ask yourself what you can do for your country. Great men are sometimes honored with public service offers as custodians of sensitive office or details of the society. A great man can be nominated to such an office or position that deals directly with the people and demand complete honesty from incorruptible men. If and when such an office or position were given to evil-minded men, the people of the society would suffer from corruption and misappropriation.

Chapter Summary

1. Great men are trustworthy
2. They are dependable
3. They are reliable
4. They have a noble character
5. They have a spirit of excellence
6. They are loving and lovable
7. They have deep knowledge and understanding

8. They get involved in running their country
9. They offer their services to their country
10. They are selfless
11. They are honest
12. They trust in the life of service

Chapter 05
The Practicality of Philip

... Let us define practicality as the quality of being realistic and the ability to act rather than talk about something.

Philip

Jesus looked up and saw that a large crowd was coming toward Him, and He said to Philip, "Where will we buy bread for these people to eat?" But He said this to test Philip, because He knew what He was about to do. Philip answered, "Two hundred denarii (200 days' wages) worth of bread is not enough for each one to receive even a little." — John 6:5-7 (AMP)

Phillip was a practical thinker who believed in acting rather than theory. Jesus asked him the question, and he gave a practical analysis of the situation. Jesus was not human but superhuman; so he knew what Philip, or any human, would say at that point in time. Jesus already knew exactly what he would do; he was about to perform another miracle of divine and exponential multiplication of physical objects to meet the needs of the needy.

Avoid Bad Compulsive Behavior

"Your beliefs become your thoughts, your thoughts become your words, your words become your actions, your actions become your habits, your habits become your values, your values become your destiny." — Mahatma Gandhi

Some people are prisoners of their compulsive or obsessive behavior, especially when shopping. They waste money and precious time on things that are unnecessary. People also prepare budgets and profit projections based on their emotions and not on reality. **The aspiring great man should be careful not to fall into the trap of wishful thinking and bloated theories** in both his life and business. He should be concerned with practical and realistic goals and not overrated projections based on unstable theories about the factors of both production and distribution. It is unwise to make decisions based on our emotions as this always ends the other way. It is best to make business decisions based on proven and verifiable facts from professional standpoints. It is better to cut off all impractical and unnecessary details from our lives and focus on essential concerns that matter. **A great man knows better than to allow himself to be dragged into unnecessary arguments with indolent and emotional freaks.** Life becomes easier and livable when we avoid disproportionate luxuries in our lives and businesses.

Work Better with Numerical Data

The great man should learn how to use the power of intuition, problem-solving skills, and creativity to adequately assess and value (or cost) products or services and analyze situations on the fly. He should be able to paint a mental picture of any situation that arises, so he can swiftly offer his opinions for the solution. Phillip the disciple was able to paint Jesus a mental picture of the least it would cost for those men, women, and children to be fed even without using a calculator or having to consult anyone. The great man should study to show himself approved by making sure he is more knowledgeable on the basics of life. **Practicality calls for the ability to be adept with numbers or numerical data**. Great men should present arguments with numbers whenever they are called upon because numbers drive the markets. This is the age of data science and everyone wants to view information in numbers and to show graphically the movements against time.

The stock market is driven by numbers and everyone all over the world watches the stock market. Investors watch to see how the markets moves up and down the chart. Every movement on the graph represents a gain or loss to people depending on where they stand on the graph. Numbers have played a major role in predictions and projections from all over the world, and recently we have noticed how numbers have affected our health in the age of COVID19.

We do not expect the numbers to be correct, but estimates, as this gives the people and decision makers an idea of what possibilities they should expect or work with. **The aspiring great man should learn how to analyze situations and give workable estimates.** This involves the ability to work with basic arithmetic including addition, multiplication, subtraction, and division to provide solutions. Phillip was able to construct a mental picture of how many people were in the crowd, how much it takes to feed one person and then multiply the cost of feeding one person by the assumed number of people in the crowd. Phillip was so practical that he even presented the estimated sum and observed a margin of error by saying that the amount was not even enough to feed everyone in the crowd. Some people consider it was an exaggeration, but of a truth it was not. The crowd was about 5000 men, (women and children were not counted, as was the tradition in the Jewish Kingdom of that day). Phillip only gave the estimate based on the number of men. He concluded by saying this amount could not go around the entire crowd if everyone were to take a bite.

Set Realizable Goals

"Cultivate the habit of setting clearly-defined written goals; they are the road maps that guide you to your destination." — Roy T. Bennett

One of the many ways great men avoid failures is to set achievable goals as opposed to excessive and unrealistic ones. Great men understand it is better to be practical and realistic in the setting of goals and budgeting. This also applies to profit projections in business ventures. A politician once announced his manifesto and promised free education, free health care and free housing to all citizens, but when asked how he would fund the projects, he could not present the numbers, he later lost out. The masses were not fooled by such empty promises and established politicians are always lying to the people merely to get the votes. **It is not mandatory to promise anything to anyone if you are not sure you can afford its execution.** Every time you make a promise, you automatically heighten the expectations of your audience and suddenly the time begins to countdown to the execution dates. **No man would accuse you of not making a promise.**

Chapter Summary

1. Great men have problem-solving skills
2. They have admirable arithmetic skills
3. They love working with numbers
4. They have the ability to draw estimates and budgets
5. They have financial calculation skills
6. They believe in reality
7. They do not make empty promises
8. They live within their means
9. They are not day dreamers
10. They do not trust in fantasy
11. They say it as it is
12. They are not excellent politicians

Chapter 06
The Integrity of Nathanael

... Let us define Integrity as the gift of divine steadfastness and moral correctness. It is the ability to stay on the right side of matters without fear or favor.

Bartholomew (Nathanael)

Nathanael answered him, "Can anything good come out of Nazareth?" Philip replied, "Come and see." Jesus saw Nathanael coming toward Him, and said of him, "Here is an Israelite indeed [a true descendant of Jacob], in whom there is no guile nor deceit nor duplicity!" -- John 1:46-47 (AMP)

Jesus announced Nathanael as an honest man, even to the bewilderment of Nathanael himself. Jesus created Nathaniel to be an honest man even before the foundation of the earth. Jesus spoke to the inner man of Nathaniel, which is the spirit. Jesus selected him as a team member to teach us that we need to be honest in all our dealings to become great in life.

Do Not Tell Lies, It Belittles You

"Above all, don't lie to yourself. The man who lies to himself and listens to his own lie comes to a point that he cannot distinguish the truth within him, or around him, and so loses all respect for himself and for others. And having no respect he ceases to love." — Fyodor Dostoyevsky

Lies are so difficult to correct. It might take a billion lies to correct one lie. You are forced to always be on guard after you lie to someone about something and are forced to lie multiple times to cover an initial lie. The aspiring great man should become an honest man in all his deeds, both in private and public spheres. He should never lie about anything for such can damage his image and reputation. **You are not mandated to please everyone simultaneously**, so you have the right to say NO to some people at some odd times in your life. Never allow yourself to be coerced or compelled into an unfavorable agreement that you do not agree with.

If your business intentionally develops products that their side effects harm the users badly and you continue selling the product, the people will eventually find out the dangers your product has caused them, and surely they will file class action lawsuits against your business. (Other lawsuits include Product Liability, Drug Recall and Medical Malpractice lawsuits etc.) This causes irreparable damage to both your personal and business reputation and negatively affects your journey up the ladder of becoming a great man.

The great man should let his Yes be yes and No be no at all times. He should not be found to be double-minded on relevant issues and critical situations. If your business sells any physical product, you should ensure the label on the product speaks the truth about the contents of your product. You should not lie on the label because it might cause damage to your users. Do not lie about the contents and raw materials used in your products as this might greatly affect your users' decision-making. Whenever the people find out about your schemes and lies, you automatically become untrustworthy and no one would depend on you anymore, thereby bringing a setback on your journey to becoming a great man.

Be Honest with Money; Pay Your Tax.

No! For unless you are honest in small matters, you won't be in large ones. If you cheat even a little, you won't be honest with greater responsibilities. And if you are untrustworthy about worldly wealth, who will trust you with the true riches of heaven? And if you are not faithful with other people's money, why should you be entrusted with money of your own? Luke 16:10-12 (TLB)

One thing that sets a great man apart from the mob is his honesty in business. He does not engage in manipulations and doctoring of legal and business documents and paperwork to his benefit. Any individual who cannot help another man up the ladder of success cannot himself become successful. You have to take great care of other people's business and money so someone else would eventually take care of yours in the future. God gives people a chance to manage mini wealth, and if they succeed, they are given more, but if not, they are stuck in the same position. One must manage his physical world as well to be successful in his spiritual life.

The great man reports and pays his taxes properly and timely; either he hires a staff to handle his taxes and accounting, or he hires a professional consulting firm to handle his books of business.

And they sent to him some of the Pharisees and some of the Herodians, to trap him in his talk. ..... Is it lawful to pay taxes to Caesar, or not? Should we pay them, or should we not?" .... Jesus said to them, "Render to Caesar the things that are Caesar's, and to God the things that are God's." - Mark 12:13-17 (ESV)

Jesus himself taught the people about taxes and taxation, even while the scholars were testing him. In his time, the Jewish nation was a province under the oppression of the Romans, and they were constantly rebelling against Roman rule and taxation. But Jesus taught them that the people should pay taxes to whoever had his image on their currency. His stance contradicted the popular belief of the radical Jews, who fought tooth and nails to stop the taxation act and who hated every one of the tax collectors for colluding with the Romans to oppress their own people.

When they came to Capernaum, the collectors of the two-drachma tax went up to Peter and said, "Does your teacher not pay the tax?" He said, "Yes." And when he came into the house, Jesus spoke to him first, saying, "What do you think, Simon? From whom do kings of the earth take toll or tax? From their sons

Be Honest with Money; Pay Your Tax.

or from others?" And when he said, "From others," Jesus said to him, "Then the sons are free. However, not to give offense to them, go to the sea and cast a hook and take the first fish that comes up, and when you open its mouth, you will find a shekel. Take that and give it to them for me and for yourself." — Matthew 17:24-27 (ESV)

Yet, in another scenario, when Peter was approached and asked about the temple taxes, he went home and Jesus instructed him to go and fish, for the first fish he will catch, has the exact amount of the needed tax money for both of them. Peter was formerly a fisherman and Jesus related to him through fishing, fish, and waters. **Jesus had the power to evade taxes, but he chose not to.** He rather decided to do as he preached and showed us how to lead by doing and not just teaching. The great man lives an exemplary life for everyone to behold his transparency. **The Great man practices exactly what he teaches, both in public and in private.** This way the great man has nothing to hide, and he is able to sleep well in his home and not hide away in hotels.

"Government's view of the economy could be summed up in a few short phrases: If it moves, tax it. If it keeps moving, regulate it. And if it stops moving, subsidize it." — Ronald Reagan

Be Positively Predictable

A great man should be positively predictable at all times. People around you should be able to predict your actions in the face of any situation. They should be able to tell what choices you will make in whatever station that will occur in the future because they already know who you are, and they know how open and honest you are.

A predictable man can easily be trusted than the unpredictable one, people can easily rest around him because they know what his line of action would be. **A man who has integrity is a man with a set of strong moral principles**. He chooses to do the right thing even in the face of temptations. He is not afraid of the outcome of his actions. This society needs more men that have high levels of integrity and are completely honest to achieve positive progress in the society.

Great men are always on the positive side of predictability. People already know what he will say to any question and as such would not approach him with immoral or evil suggestions, because they know he will always say no to anything that is not positive and anything that does not protect the helpless and minorities in the society. It will be absolutely difficult for evil men to approach you and try to convert you to become evil. Wicked people will always avoid you because they know you will always say no to their ways or will simply disapprove of their actions.

Be Morally Correct

One of the rules of greatness you still adopt the principles of integrity and complete honesty. **You can never become a great man if you are not honest in all your ways**. You would have to be morally correct in all your dealings with people, both indoors and outdoors, in secret and in open. It involves living a simple life without having evil secrets. **You should be the same person in your bedroom and in the public marketplace**. This means you should never lead a double life; people should know you for who you are at all times. You should also be yourself both in the king's present and the beggar in the street. A man of integrity does not join a group of people who support immoral acts irrespective of who is involved. They do not support any group or groups of people who revel in immorality. They speak out whenever their colleagues or friends decide to go the immoral way. They openly boycott relationships with people who rejoice in immorality and do not allow themselves to be dragged into any act or form of immorality.

It is true that the world does not always like the men of integrity. **The entire world hates honest people**. If you therefore want to be a great man in life, you should be ready to face these challenges and prosecutions. Be prepared to face unpleasant situations because your family, friends and loved ones would desert you soon. You might become very lonely, but do not regret your stance because we need people like you in the society, for the society to become a better one.

Chapter Summary

1. Great men are honest
2. They pay their fair share of taxes
3. They are not scammers
4. They do not lie
5. They do not manipulate people
6. Their word is their life
7. They have their functional moral compass intact
8. They have a conscience
9. They are dependable followers and servants
10. They are predictable
11. They fight immorality
12. **They face many persecutions**

Chapter 07
The Skepticism of Thomas

... Let us define Skepticism as the act of questioning any fact before making informed decisions.

Thomas (Didymus)

So the other disciples kept telling him, "We have seen the Lord!" But he said to them, "Unless I see in His hands the marks of the nails, and put my finger into the nail prints, and put my hand into His side, I will never believe." - John 20:25 (AMP)

Thomas was a man with a skeptical attitude and accepted only what he could see. He sought for proof and evidence for any fact. He maintained that resurrection was impossible, so he wanted to witness a physical evidence before accepting.

This is a controversial trait and value to be included here as a disciple or principle for greatness. Jesus did not make any mistake in including someone with a skeptical attitude as one of his disciples. Jesus wants his followers to explore constructive skepticism (the positive side) to our advantage. The Apostle John instructed in 1 John 4:1 (KJV) and said: "Beloved, believe not every spirit, but try the spirits whether they are of God: because many false prophets are gone out into the world". Jesus knew there will be a worse case of scam artists at the end time than what they witnessed in his lifetime. There were people who went about doing miracles even in the name of Jesus who were not his disciples.

Think for Yourself

The positive value I am bringing out here is the ability to think-for-yourself. In this book I refer to it as the natural and unwritten of law of the thought process: Personalization-of-Thought. Our society is filled with stereotypes and bias resulting from racism, segregation, and marginalization. **The great man must learn how to personalize his thoughts and never go with the flow.** Never let the society think for you because you are unique, and every situation you meet is unique and must not be generalized into a stereotype.

Create and Apply A Skeptic-Filter

The sub section of society that think for some people include but not limited to the: Television, radio, Internet, Social media, public opinion, unions, schools and colleges, teachers, religious leaders, politicians, advocacy groups, influential people, your parents, activists and peer groups. The solution here is to create the skeptic-filter for everything you hear or perceive. The skeptic-filter is your buffer, which filters out obscene thoughts, facts and lies from everything you hear or see. It allows absolute truth through but after a careful test by fire.

Question and Fact-Check Everything

The fiery filtering process includes questioning, vetting, and fact-checking of everything you see or hear to determine their worthiness and authenticity. You must question everything you hear, vet any situation you interface with, and fact-check every story that involves you.

Constructive skepticism is the skeptical attitude of not believing everything you see or hear or see, especially in the news (TV or Radio) until you see tangible evidence. You should verify everything you hear, read between lines, and make sure they are tangible. Do not accept everything you read on the internet either.

Do Not Believe the Internet

The internet is an open source environment and lacks censorship. Anyone from anywhere can post anything including but not limited to articles, blogs, videos etc. **Lately, the internet has become the stage for scams and hoaxes**. There are myriads of cases where the internet has been used to harm innocent people, including but not limited to; money scams, Ponzi schemes, fake news, fake products, get-rich-quick, identity theft, fake or doctored product reviews, etc. It would be beneficial to not trust anything you see on the internet at first until you fact-check such against other outlets and the origins of such information.

Below are biblical references to support the fact that you should not trust any fact until you have more sources as witnesses.

> *"A single witness shall not rise up against a man on account of any iniquity or any sin which he has committed; on the evidence of two or three witnesses a matter shall be confirmed. Deuteronomy 19:15*
>
> *Do not receive an accusation against an elder except on the basis of two or three witnesses. 1 Timothy 5:19*

Most information on the internet is meant to deceive you into making impulsive decisions which would end in damage to your personality, trust, and finances. Sometimes the internet has commercials that try to sell you something you never needed, fake products or fake business ventures or jobs. It is better to sometimes install some software on your browser that would block all ads because most of them are malicious and would only cause you pain.

You should ask many questions and seek for documented and verified proof and evidence to support any claim or fact before you consider such. Do not be hasty in accepting any information on the internet, but give it a third, fourth and fifth thoughts and wait a little longer before going on with any action plan. Time will always tell; still holds true to verifying any obtrusive claim.

Do Not Trust Every News on TV

The great man does not trust any headline, especially captivating, enticing, and seductive ones. The writers, over the ages, have learned to use such tempting headlines to arrest the attention of innocent people and force them to give a second look into their stories. The great man should look at the source of the information and if it is not from a well censored source, then squash it. He digs deeper into any story before he considers it believable.

When you need to watch or listen to the news even on TV; make sure it is the news section that you listen to and not the talk shows. **The talk shows are not news but personal opinions** of the talk show host. You do not have to listen to any of them because they always talk about their personal opinions and beliefs. They also condemn other people's opinions and beliefs. They always tout their beliefs as the perfect one and want you to trust and follow them. But you have the choice either to listen to them or not.

Get Daily Reports

One way to effectively manage a business is to demand for daily reports from different employees on the same issues. Make sure the reports are not the same but unique. The goal is to confirm their honesty. The great man should not always believe any report on-the-fly, even from his most trusted employees. You need to sit down and go through the data line by line for yourself and ask questions, because when the chips go down, the burden will always fall on your shoulders while the employees would always leave for other jobs elsewhere. Compare the original reports to determine if anyone is manipulating any data in your business.

The great man does not always go along with the public on matters. He digs into any cause to find the underlying truth in the matter before he takes his decision. He does not take sides with the masses too; he does not engage in conspiracy theories and myths but carves out a path for himself. Brilliant investors get daily reports on the economy and stock market to enable them to stay abreast with the trends. You should know about the daily progress of your business and economy to enable you to make informed decisions in life and business. Find out who is losing and gaining in business and tailor your decision to accommodate such.

Apply Selective Lifestyle Formula

The selective lifestyle formula is a derivative of my 6 Laws of Selectivity, among my Natural and Unwritten Laws of Common Sense. **This law states that a great man chooses what he perceives from his senses**, whatever he needs or approves, and then ignores or blocks whatever he does not need or approve at a certain point in time. The truth is you will never go extremely far in life if you accept every information the society throws at you without a form of censorship. Through this law, you can listen to everything in your society but train your senses to block out the undesirable information without taking them to heart. It has to do with the ability to control and condition your mind to listen to you.

So, it is all about the daily training and renewal of your mind, which is your sole responsibility. You have the instinctive power to control your sense of sight, hearing, smell, taste, touch and spirit by choosing what you see, hear, smell, taste, touch or feel in the face of multitudes of freely available data and information overload.

Chapter Summary

1. Great men are not easily fooled
2. They are not candidates for scammers
3. They believe only what has logical proof

Apply Selective Lifestyle Formula

4. They have their opinions
5. They sometimes seem difficult to convince
6. They love reading charts and numbers
7. They are reluctant to join a revolution
8. They are willing to give more time for fact checking
9. They question everything
10. They take absolute control of their minds
11. They chose what they hear
12. They chose what they perceive

Chapter 08
The Discipline of Matthew

... Let us define discipline as the act of strictly injecting correctness in a wrongdoer by open rebuke as a means of stifling unacceptable behavior.

Matthew (Levi, the tax collector)

And after these things he went forth, and beheld a publican, named Levi, sitting at the place of toll, and said unto him, Follow me. — Luke 5:27 (ASV)

The Bible expressly teaches discipline and says in Proverbs 23:13-14 (NIV): *Do not withhold discipline from a child; if you punish them with the rod, they will not die. Punish them with the rod and save them from death.* It is also recorded in Proverbs 29:15 (NIV) that: *A rod and a reprimand impart wisdom, but a child left undisciplined, disgraces its mother.* Discipline is inevitable in the life of humans because we sometimes act selfishly, and the repercussion of such acts often means danger to other innocent people. The prison system is a form of discipline for criminals and it is mostly for the undisciplined people of the society.

Jesus called a tax collector as a disciple and received backlash because the Jews at the time condemned the tax collectors who oppressed the people and forcefully collected taxes for the Romans. Levi was a man who handled public money, or a tax gatherer. He was in active service for the oppressor. He was not a fisherman like most of the disciples were. Just like the IRS, tax collectors were prone to using force to compel the people to comply with the rules of taxation. This made them appear like cruel taskmasters, tyrants, or authoritarian slave drivers. It was a demanding job for Levi and anyone in his position to be perceived as a traitor by his people. He was one of the people used by the oppressors to force the people to pay taxes or obey their rules. Tax collectors can go to any length to recover unpaid taxes and this power and authority forces people to avoid the trouble of losing all their wealth to these tax gatherers by paying their taxes duly and on time.

Adopt a Disciplined Life

The keyword here is to become a disciplinarian. The great man should practice firm discipline at all times. **Many souls have been lost in our society because we have forgotten the role of discipline in our lives and society at large.** The aspiring great man should himself be a disciplined person who has absolute control over his faculties, emotions, and habits. He should be regarded as an example in the society. He should teach and instill a sense of discipline in his followers and employees. Every wrongdoing or evil should be called out, and the doer punished as a deterrent to others. **Self-indulgence, extravagance, and profuse wantonness should not be tolerated at any level because they can result in a failure to attain potential success.**

A life of discipline is synonymous with accountability. It makes the society regard someone as one of its great people. To be disciplined means one does not get himself or herself involved with immoral acts that can lead to crime. Discipline helps correct bad behavior and every great man should learn how to apply it to check his own life and behavior.

Avoid Discrimination and Segregation

Jesus selected him into his camp to prove to us that we need to accept everyone and shun all forms of discrimination, segregation, and racism. The society hated people like Mathew mostly for what they did for a living, but Jesus selected him due to who he was.

Great men gaze beyond the ordinary and see people for who they are and not what they do or where they come from. Every human has positive values if we can get to know them personally. Great men do not see another human through the color of their skins, the texture of their hairs, the accent in their voice, their country of birth, or their physical beauty and shortcomings. Every individual's personality is not written on his face. **The proper man of a man is the man inside the man.**

Disregard Beauty for Character

The aspiring great man should learn how to relate to people for who they really are. Looks are deceptive and causes many people to make errors in their decision. People sometimes prefer people who are tall, slim, athletic, light-skinned, narrow waist, V-shaped torso, broad shoulders, straight and slender legs, suntanned skin, narrow face, less fat, narrow eyebrows, longer lashes, high cheekbones, full breasts, full lips, big thighs, etc. All these are but temporal features of people, and they change with time and circumstances. The actual person is inside the body and will remain even after those sexy features drop off with age or circumstance.

Great men do not allow sexual attraction to cloud their reasoning when making choices because they understand eventually those qualities will evaporate.

Chapter Summary

1. Great men are disciplined people
2. They are in control of their emotions
3. They are not moved by surface values of objects, people, and situations
4. They can hold public offices well
5. They do not discriminate
6. They do not segregate

7. They treat and regard all as equal
8. They extend equal opportunities to everyone
9. They believe in the positive values of people
10. They are ready to do the right thing and face persecution
11. They entertain no amount of fear
12. **They strongly believe in constituted authority**

Chapter 09
The Anonymity of James

... Let us define anonymity as the conscious effort to hide from undue attention and publicity.

James ("Son of Alphaeus") the younger

But when you give to charity, do not let your left hand know what your right hand is doing, so that your deeds of charity may be in secret; and your Father, who sees in secret will reward you openly.-Matthew 6:3-4 (AMPC)

James (the younger) was the most obscure of all the disciples. There are no references in the Bible about what he said or did. This does not mean he was less than a disciple. He was equal to the rest but was absolutely not the attention seeking fellow. You might wonder why Jesus selected a man who was so quiet and uneventful to join his team, but after much meditation I got this answer, anonymity.

Great men Prefer to Remain Anonymous

People who aspire to be great are always on the other side of anonymity, they prefer to be flamboyant and loud. People want to always become and remain the center of attraction and attention as their petty formula to achieve greatness. They demand the needy people sing their praises in the streets and worship them as a god for them to be helped. But after this revelation about James the Less, I now understand that genuine great men try as much as possible to remain anonymous and avoid undue publicity.

The aspiring great man should realize some scenarios where he should remain anonymous. In the area of giving back to the society, he can offer magnanimous gifts and remain anonymous. This does not make him less than a great man.

Do Not Be Boastful

Then he said to me, "This is the word of the Lord to Zerubbabel: Not by might, nor by power, but by my Spirit, says the Lord of hosts. Zechariah 4:6 (ESV)

The great man is a man of humble spirit, and he is not interested in trading his humility for wealth. He serves the people with love and respect and does not assume that he is better or higher than the next Joe. The great man should avoid pride like a plaque, for it is a sure step towards a fall. **The habit of remaining anonymous helps you overcome pride** and unnecessary attention, which can cause you to puff up.

Boasting diminishes humans to a thing worse than dirt and dust. Whenever you boast, you lose a positive step in life which in turn diminishes your personality exponentially. When you become a proud and boastful man, you take glory for your successes and you tell the world that your entire success is due to your education and hard work. But God is the only one who distributes favor. Success comes from God's favor and not from human efforts, power, intellect, or might.

Practice Selflessness

"Every man must decide whether he will walk in the light of creative altruism or in the darkness of destructive selfishness." — Martin Luther King Jr.

The success of the great man is also defined by his selfless efforts and disposition. The aspiring Great man must offer his services to humanity out of his own volition and without demanding for favors in return. Anonymity is illuminated in selflessness. The great man should present himself or his finances to help whenever the society is in dire need, as in cases of emergency or war and strife. He should not hold back his wealth at these times because this is the season God raised him up to shine. **He should be ready to shine his light for the society when there is darkness around the people.**

Great men go the extra mile to be of help to their people and seldom go public on whom they help and what amount they spend to help the needy in the society. They should not brag about their offering because if they do, they will lose their blessing from God.

Great men should avoid helping anyone with the sole aim of earning a praise or favor. Help should be rendered when you are comfortable to help and not when coerced. Martin Luther King Jr. concluded that. "An individual has not started living until he can rise above the narrow confines of his individualistic concerns to the broader concerns of all humanity."

Chapter Summary

1. Great men prefer to remain anonymous
2. Great men avoid the limelight
3. They are not proud
4. They are not boastful
5. They do not ask to be praised or worshiped
6. They are selfless
7. They are neither envious nor jealous
8. They secretly wish other people well

9. They humble
10. They silently support the helpless in the society
11. They believe in the equality of humans
12. They work behind the scenes

Chapter 10
The Zeal of Jude

... Let us define Zeal as the conscious and compulsive effort to accomplish one's task, purpose or destiny.

Jude (Judas, Thaddaeus, Lebbeus); also called "the Zealot"

Judas (not Iscariot) asked Him, "Lord, what has happened that You are going to reveal Yourself to us and not to the world?" — John 14:22 (AMP)

Thaddaeus was one disciple who is said to have belonged to the Zealot political movement in that era. They were constantly trying to resist the Romans, who were their colonial masters. Thaddeus was interested in making Jesus Christ known to the entire world as their warrior messiah and ruling king to be feared. He had so much passion for his people and wanted to do anything in his power to liberate them from the Romans, even by physical war.

Develop Passion for Your Society

Thaddaeus and his group thought Jesus was the warring messiah like King David, and they expected him to usher in world peace through war with the Romans, just as the prophet Isaiah said in his prophecy. That is why he asked Jesus when he will reveal himself to the world. To Thaddaeus, Jesus would help establish the political authority of the Jews and restore their sovereignty over their enemies and oppressors who were the Romans of his day. Jesus Christ was not sent to fight any physical war, he came to establish a new covenant which involved the emancipation of the mind, spiritual freedom, and love for enemies. But he will certainly wage physical war on earth when he comes back the second time to establish world peace.

"Nothing great in the world was accomplished without passion." — Georg Wilhelm Friedrich Hegel

---

The great man in the making should develop love and passion for his community and their people, his job, and fellow humans. He should zealously or passionately seek to make his world and community a better place for everyone living there and the world at large. He should never be self-centered but passionate about supporting positive development in his community. He should be passionate about his business and his employees; by only going into the type of business he loves, and not a type of business that he does for the money.

A great man's passion to help the minority in the community would eventually accelerate his movement up the ladder of success. **It is a golden rule for someone to do well and with passion whatever he must do.** Maya Angelou once said, "You can only become truly accomplished at something you love. Don't make money your goal. Instead pursue the things you love doing and then do them so well that people can't take their eyes off of you."

The great man should discover his passions earlier in life, even before college, if he must go to college. Your passion is your life's purpose and will lead you to your destiny as a joyful man. What are the things that make you happy in life? Develop and major in them and you will remain a joyful individual in life. Never get involved in a trade for the sole purpose of the money or prestige, for you will live a miserable life thereafter. I have seen many students complete college in a discipline and return to college to read another discipline entirely.

Some read a course in an A sector in college but worked in a B sector after college without applying what they read in college for work.

Be Diligent in Your Work

> *"If a man is called to be a street sweeper, he should sweep streets even as a Michelangelo painted, or Beethoven composed music or Shakespeare wrote poetry. He should sweep streets so well that all the hosts of heaven and earth will pause to say, 'Here lived a great street sweeper who did his job well."* —
> *Martin Luther King Jr.*

Diligence (careful and persistent work or effort) is also a factor for greatness in this discipline. You should do all you have to do diligently, and over time you would surely reap the fruits of your labor. You might have to work late, work under rain or sun, and work with an empty stomach or under oppression, but if you continue and complete your work, then greatness awaits you. I should mention **that working diligently in this age involves working smart and not working hard**; literally. It involves working with smart tools and technology to accomplish so much in a noticeably brief period.

> *Do you see a man diligent and skillful in his business? He will stand before kings; he will not stand before obscure men.* — *Proverbs 22:29 (AMPC)*

When you combine both zeal (passion) with diligence in your life, the rewards will certainly raise you to deal with kings and queens of the world. You will dominate your peers and competitors. People all over the world will know your name for good and will desire work with you on many matters. You will become a magnet for myriads of opportunities globally. Your growth and profits will rise exponentially and so your enemies. Money would then become your servant at this level because of the much wealth that would be given to you even as a gift; wealth you never worked for or gained from your sweat. Ralph Waldo Emerson once said, "Nothing great was ever achieved without enthusiasm."

Become a Man of Hope

.... A man with a desire for favorable outcomes.

The man who is aspiring to become a great man should not lose hope on his society irrespective of whatever is going on at the moment. He does not lose hope on his employees or business even when it seems like everything is closing down. He keeps hope alive, especially when the chips are down, and he encourages his colleagues and friends to also keep hope alive.

> *"If you lose hope, somehow you lose the vitality that keeps moving, you lose that courage to be, that quality that helps you go on in spite of it all. And so today I still have a dream."* — Martin Luther King Jr.

He is a confidant person and someone everyone can look up to when they are at their lowest point in life. **The great man gives hope to the hopeless**, and he restores the faith of depressed people around him. From time to time in any society comes a time when everyone would lose hope and some would even go down the inglorious path of suicide, but the great man is the one who volunteers to speak to the people and encourage them to hold on for just a little longer. The great man does not give up on people, but he finds positive values in everyone around him, irrespective of any actions they might have been involved in their past lives.

The great man believes every human being has innate positive values embedded in them that should be discovered. Often these values are overshadowed by evil habits that corrupt their minds. Sometimes these habits are picked up from their interactions with their environments and associates, as it is often said that evil association corrupts good habits. **The great man avoids evil association with delinquent friends** and company that can corrupt their ethical habits and overshadow their positive values. **The great man does not give up on people and their governments even when they are seemingly on a wrong path. These men take their time to pray for their leaders in authority and then ask God to intervene and surely, God always does.**

They are not a party to evil in their society and certainly not a part of the problem of the society, but they are the troubleshooters and solution providers to the society's ills.

Aspire and Become a Man of Faith

... A man with a blank and compulsive belief in desirable outcomes from his God. He believes in the supernatural as the controller of all situations.

A great man believes in God. He believes God created the heavens and the Earth and that God is in absolute control of everything on Earth. He believes everything that happens today has been written down through the power of the Holy Spirit by prominent apostles and prophets of old. He believes we are not in absolute control or everything, but that God is.

He believes in Jesus Christ as the son of God and our savior. Faith in God is like believing in the impossible or believing in a lie that cannot be proven. It looks absurd to have faith in God, but it is worth it, even when we understand a little about God, and we cannot see him, we still believe whatever is written about him.

We have different names for God in different tribes and tongues globally. The general idea is, God is the supernatural being who works behind the scenes in our lives, universe and situations.

Embrace Optimism

"I am fundamentally an optimist. Whether that comes from nature or nurture, I cannot say. Part of being optimistic is keeping one's head pointed toward the sun, one's feet moving forward. There were many dark moments when my faith in humanity was sorely tested, but I would not and could not give myself up to despair. That way lays defeat and death." — Nelson Mandela

Optimism in this book refers to the belief in an impossible positive outcome and the ignorance of prevalent negative facts. A great man is a man who has a passion for whatever he does, and he sure believes the cup is rather half full. He is optimistic about life, irrespective of present or prevalent circumstances. He hopes for the best and simultaneously prepares for the worst. He is unperturbed about negative circumstances and pessimistic people around him but focuses on the brighter side of things and believes the storm will soon be over. He also believes whatever has a beginning must surely have an ending. You have to always look at the brighter outcome of events to become a great man. It is in this regard that a great man can become a leader.

As a leader, you have to develop this belief in the positive side of people, not condemning and dehumanizing them irrespective of their actions. You have to learn how to encourage other people to become their best, especially in times of distress and depression.

Exercise Some Patience

Patience in this book refers to **the ability to comfortably hold on to unfavorable situations for just a little longer**. Patience is an immensely powerful tool for anyone who must succeed in life and become great. The gap between hope and manifestation is the most tempting season of human life. It is during this period that evil seduces the weak-minded people with temptations through their cravings and lustful desires.

I have seen and heard of many people who gave up at the eleventh hour to their success. It pays to have a little more patience on any matter in life, including but not limited to life decisions, choices, and contracts. The great man must have enough patience with situations and people around him. Do not make decisions and choices in a haste, give it a little more time, sleep over it, or take a minute and drink a glass of water before you commit yourself to any serious matter.

Pay Attention to Detail

This refers to the ability to be fully aware of one's environment. It requires one to paint a mental picture of everything around him or her. You should learn and watch out for unusual or criminal behavior, take note of the faces of people around you, watch for suspicious faces or motives. Check yourself if you are vulnerable to attacks, hide your personal stuff like wallets and cellphones. Secure your bag and other vulnerable items on your person. Adopt a safe position wherever you are; by backing a wall and facing the exit when sitting or standing, this way someone cannot jump you easily. If you find yourself in an uncomfortable environment, take a leave and look for someplace else. Be careful about interacting with strangers, for you cannot trust anyone you have never met before. Make sure you do not become a nuisance to others in public.

Focus on Your Life's Purpose & Destiny

"Knowing yourself is the beginning of all wisdom." — *Aristotle*

Your purpose and destiny are the two most important things in your life, you must guard them dearly. **Your life's purpose is your mission statement or short-term goal, while your destiny is your vision statement or long-term goal.** Just like mission is the action that produces the vision, your life's purpose is your tool for achieving your destiny. Your life becomes a waste whenever you deviate from your pre-destined route for something else.

You must be aware of the fact that your purpose and destiny are unique to you and to you only. This means you must never compare yourself or your progress in life to another individual. There is absolutely no correlation between your destiny and your brother, sister, or classmate. Nature brings people together for them to learn and share a thing or two along their life's journey, but never to force them into one route or merge their destinies.

I have said earlier that your college education can interfere with your destiny, if you ever find that out on time, please do yourself a favor and either ignore the particular course of dropout completely. We should regard education as a tool that helps us fulfill our destinies and not to create new destinies for us or control us.

You should never surrender your power to scholars but control what you learn and only focus on whatever advances your destiny. Life is too short for someone to waste a greater part of his life to learn useless knowledge. Do not abandon your destiny to pursue money but focus on your destiny and money will meet you along the way.

"Excellence is never an accident. It is always the result of high intention, sincere effort, and intelligent execution; it represents the wise choice of many alternatives – choice, not chance, determines your destiny." — Aristotle

Your talents are those divine tools that are implanted in you that you need to implement in order to arrive at your destiny. A great man is a man who has discovered his talents or life's purposes in life without which he cannot start living. We can only start living when we discover and exploit our God-given talents to execute our life's purposes, which finally lead to our fulfilled destiny.

Greatness involves a clear knowledge of who you are (Self-knowledge and mastery), where you come from (your origins, past), where you are (your position, present), why you do what you do (your reasoning) and where you are headed (your destination, your future). It is after one understands these things about himself that he can then develop zeal or passion for his talents.

Develop a Passion for Service to Customers

Customers are the most important assets of any business and it is advisable for any entrepreneur to develop passion to serve its customers. The profit of any business is directly proportional to the number of satisfied customers it has. The more customers you have, the more profits you are likely to gain. You cannot have more customers if you cannot satisfy the first few, and when you satisfy your customers by serving them well, you will have more customers coming back, and this translates to more profit.

Let us consider the CEO of Amazon.com. Jeff Bezos decided to build Amazon.com to primarily serve the public find books on the internet. He built the business and made sure the customer always comes first. The customer obsession is his number one principle to success at Amazon.com, which now offers Amazon Prime, a paid membership service that offers so many benefits including same-day, one-day, and free shipping to its customers. You can buy an item in the morning and get it delivered on the same day. There are also free movies and music apps that can help its customers cut-the-cable. This same day shipping model does not seem to fetch Amazon.com much profit, but it sure gets them more customers.

Chapter Summary

1. Great men discover who they are,
2. They discover their past
3. Great men discover their present
4. They discover their future

5. Great men focus on their life's purposes and destiny
6. Great men are passionate about their destiny
7. They are diligent in all their work
8. They are optimistic about life
9. They have patience
10. They pay great attention to details
11. They are aware of their location
12. They help other people achieve their destinies too

Chapter 11
The Patriotism of Simon

... Let us define Patriotism as the love and dedication to one's country and countrymen. It involves the practice and assurance of equality before the law.

Simon ("the Canaanite") also called "the Zealot"

Simon was another disciple who is said to have belonged to the Zealot political movement. The Zealots were Jews who were rebelling against Roman rule and taxation. They were an aggressive political party whose concern for the national and religious life of the Jewish people led them to despise even Jews who sought peace and conciliation with the Roman authorities.

Love Your Nation & People

Patriotism here refers to being full of love for one's country, and it involves serving your country to the best of your knowledge and power. The act of waving of the flag is also associated with patriotism. We want to focus on patriotism as any act that strengthens your country. This chapter will explore the benefits of the legislative service of great men. Loyalty to your nation and your leaders is also an act of patriotism and is to be observed properly.

Every nation that should prosper in goodness needs the support of all its ethical people to join in the affairs and legislation of the nation. The great man will have to also contribute to the development and ruling of his country. I know many principled people never want to go into politics for fear of persecution. This decision is detrimental to the health of any nation, which would now be left in the hands of wicked people. The evil people are left to rule the good people, and they are given the power to force their wickedness, evil and immorality and whatever they want over the people. **The only solution to sanitize a nation is to vote out all evil and wicked people from all positions of authority and power.** This is a Herculean task, but it is not impossible. The trustworthy great men of a nation would have to gather and decide to begin this rigorous journey. They should start from the grassroots and climb up the ladder until they get to the apex of the legislature, the judiciary, and the executive arms of governance.

This is not a short-term ordeal but a long-term saga; so they should not be in a hurry. The keyword here is for the principled men to take back the power and authority from the wicked men in authority of their society. **When the evil men rule a country, the people will be oppressed and destroyed,** and there will be no one to fight their cause. It is rather impossible to get justice from a wicked rule when all the sectors of governance are controlled by the wicked who are in immoral agreement and partnership. How then will an innocent man get justice if all the arms of governance, including the executive, legislative and judiciary, all collude together and eat from the same plate? The answer is 'No way!'

The collusion of the arms of governance of any community exterminates both the laws of segregation of powers and the principle of checks and balances, which inadvertently destroys the hope for justice for the powerless and the innocent of the society. The people are subject to the oppression and injustice from their evil and immoral rulers in such a compromised generation.

Go Vote and Be Voted For

Exemplary men need to vote and be voted for, in order to make the society a better place for everyone. Unselfish men need to also aspire to become lawmakers of the land by getting involved. They can start from city commissions and councils to a federal legislature. Legislators are men who are elected by the public to work at various levels of government, and they belong to the legislative arm of any government. The legislature is responsible for enacting new laws and amending existing ones.

The legislators govern by proposing new bills, holding votes, and passing new laws. If most of the legislators were oppressors, evil, wicked and immoral men, they would only propose new laws that would suit their way of life and business, and their accomplices to the disadvantages of the honest and innocent of the society.

"Our lives begin to end the day we become silent about things that matter." — Martin Luther King Jr.

The innocent citizens would always remain the victims of these laws instituted by immoral men. Even when the wicked men commit crimes, they amend the laws to accommodate their lifestyle and wrongdoing because there are no unselfish men in the legislature to fight back or bring them to justice. The masses suffer and continue groaning and murmuring in their homes if they could ever afford one.

The wicked men eventually take everything that belongs to the common people as their own, including land and other resources, leaving the people destitute and broke. Equality then becomes a thing of the past and a myth. The evil men eventually become like gods and ask to be worshiped. They demand for the people to beg them for food and shelter in return for obeisance.

It is clearly written in the book of Proverbs 29:2 (AMP) that "When the righteous are in authority and become great, the people rejoice; But when the wicked man rules, the people groan and sigh."

Fight for Equal Rights & Justice

> *"We must take sides. Neutrality helps the oppressor, never the victim. Silence encourages the tormentor, never the tormented. Sometimes we must interfere. When human lives are endangered, when human dignity is in jeopardy, national borders and sensitivities become irrelevant. Wherever men and women are persecuted because of their race, religion, or political views, that place must – at that moment – become the center of the universe."*— Elie Wiesel

The fate of any nation depends entirely on its patriots, who are bold enough to challenge the injustice of these oppressors and bring about freedom and emancipation of the masses.

This war is not without its downsides and casualties, but persistence will always get the job done. The casualties should not deter the great men but continue in the fight for the emancipation of their people. There would still be casualties when there are no champions who decide to stand up and fight. The oppressors would still destroy more lives and get away with it.

> *"We know through painful experience that freedom is never voluntarily given by the oppressor; it must be demanded by the oppressed."* Martin Luther King Jr

Martin Luther King Jr. was an ordinary man who took on this war like a man. He fought the war until he was no more. But no other great man has been fighting like he did. If we had at least one great man like MLK in every state of the nation fighting with him and after him to this day, this country would have been rid of oppressors from every level. Where are the MLKs of this generation?

Nelson Mandela contributed to the freedom and emancipation of his people, but how many Mandelas do we have today who are willing to stand up and fight for the emancipation of their generation?

The only tool to fight the war of inequality and emancipation today is a legislative service of many faithful and great men of the society. You can either rise, fight, and die fighting to liberate your generation, or agree to stay alive and be enslaved, oppressed, and finally killed (condemning your generation to eternal slavery). The choice is yours. Either way, no one will live forever on earth.

Chapter Summary

1. Great men love their countries
2. They love their fellow countrymen
3. They believe in the greatness of their country
4. They accept everyone in their country as brothers and sisters
5. They vote and are voted for
6. They fight against oppression
7. They fight against injustice
8. They speak out whenever they see any instance of dehumanization
9. They respect other countries too
10. They do not support war and destruction of other humans
11. They also vote in the election of county and city officials
12. They believe in the dignity of all persons

Chapter 12
The Frugality of Judas

... Let us define frugality as the compulsive habit of living only on one's basic needs and avoiding the wasteful life of luxury.

Judas Iscariot (the betrayer)

But one of His disciples, Judas Iscariot, Simon's son, who would betray Him, said, "Why was this fragrant oil not sold for three hundred denarii and given to the poor?" This he said, not that he cared for the poor, but because he was a thief, and had the money box; and he used to take what was put in it. — John 12:4-6 (NKJV)

Avoid The 'Love' of Money

Judas had many character traits and among them were betrayal, envy, greed, and theft. I want you to overlook all those undesirable traits for once and focus on one positive value and principle that is superficially convincing about him. Judas pretended to be a frugal man and not wasteful, even if he did not mean it, we can still attribute that to him because he mentioned it.

Judas was the treasurer for the team, and it seems he was able to do that job to the best of his ability as a thief. Jesus knew who he was and what he could do, so he allowed him to hold the money bag. His selection was not for him to contribute positively to the group but to be the betrayer, as was his destiny. He had the love for money which blinded his judgment, so Jesus allowed him to handle the money just to make him happy. Judas was the only man created to become the betrayer of the Messiah and if he did not complete his job, there would have been no salvation to mankind and Jesus's mission would not have been complete. Great men do not love money. They apply the unwritten laws of frugality to overcome the love of money and control money instead of being controlled by money.

Delay Gratification (Dave Chappelle Style)

Delayed gratification is the satisfaction postponed to a later date when one would rather be in a better position to enjoy such and stay alive and correct. Success comes at different levels of people's lives and often it destroys many who are not ready to handle such at that particular time of their lives. It is best to postpone such to a later date when one must have attained both emotional and spiritual maturity enough to handle such tremendous success.

Dave Chappelle is an African American stand-up comedian who walked away from a whopping $50 million contract around 2005 but received a mouthwatering $60 million and more from Netflix for a 3-in-1 comedy-special contract deal in 2016. He successfully applied the natural and unwritten laws of delayed gratification amidst brutal speculation and national uproar. Dave is my favorite comedian and I love listening to his jokes about politics, racism, and African American culture. After watching his interview with Oprah on YouTube, I was convinced that I was not in error. He explained to Oprah the reason he walked away from the said money and I give him kudos for exhibiting such a high level of ethics and professionalism.

OPRAH WINFREY: Everybody wants to know why d'you walk away from $50 million?

DAVE CHAPPELLE: Well, I wasn't walking away from the money... I was walking away from the circumstances that were coming with the newfound plateau... And I felt like, in a lot of instances, I was deliberately being put through stress... Because, you know, when you're a guy that generates money, people have a vested interest in controlling you... I'm telling you; I was incredibly stressed out; you know... I was doing sketches that were funny, but socially irresponsible... I felt like I was deliberately being encouraged, and I was overwhelmed... So it's like you're getting flooded with things, and you don't pay attention to things like your ethics or when you get so overwhelmed... It's like you had won the lottery.

Source: Why Comedian Dave Chappelle Walked Away From $50 million | The Oprah Winfrey Show | OWN

(www.youtube.com/watch?v=tlScX2stRuo)

Stop Wastefulness

The great man should learn how not to be wasteful for any reason. He should focus on his needs and not wants. He should not live a flamboyant life because it is wasteful and might put him in trouble. It is not the best to go with the flow of things in the society like fashion, automobiles etc. just for the show or the fun of it. It is an absolutely genuine statement that being frugal can help you become rich in life. The golden rule of amassing riches is to spend less than you earn and invest the difference. And it is frugality that can help you spend less than you earn. Frugality also affords you more money for investment. Mark me, when I say frugality, I do not mean to be stingy; for both are quite different words with different meanings.

The frugal man is someone who is incredibly careful about how he spends his money. He lives an unusually simple, uncomplicated, and prudent life. The stingy man refers to someone who is unwilling to spend money even on his needs and when it matters. The stingy man never gives gifts or financial support to other people, but the frugal man does.

Do Not Support Abusive Habits

The frugal man supports other people financially, even to a fault, but not just anyone who asks for money. He investigates and verifies you are really in need and you will use the money for whatever you claim, which must be a need and not a terrible habit. He does not support abusive behaviors and habits that can endanger the body, the environment, and other humans. After helping someone financially, he also offers valuable counsel and advice to make sure the individual's situation changes from a beggar to a giver, thereby empowering the individual to be in a position to help others in need.

Frugality is about prioritizing your spending. It involves focusing on essential needs and investing the rest of the balance back into your businesses. You can also save a portion of the balance for almsgiving and community service. Frugality is the major key to financial freedom. It gives you much more money for investments, especially in autopilot and diversified methods.

Take Control Over Money

Frugality gives you control over money. When you restrict the way you spend money, you are in control over money, and money cannot control you. On the other way around, if you are not in control of your money when you suddenly make a colossal sum of money, you might waste it on unnecessary things, and after a while, the money disappears and leaves you in debt. Frugality helps you keep track of your spending; you will be able to document all your spending. At the end of the year you would surely understand how much money you earned and spent on different areas of your life. Frugality helps keep you healthy. When you live a frugal life, you will surely avoid eating junk food and only eat home-cooked food, which is better for your health. This cuts you off from the dangers of junk food including excessive sugar, sodium, and food preservatives. Frugality also puts you in control over food.

Live Above Debt

Frugality causes you live above debt. Many people lust after every brand new and latest car of their fancy, and they end up wasting so much money on its maintenance and forget the value of the car would diminish over time. The periodic payments including full coverage insurance premiums can be saved and re-invested in your business when you are satisfied with a reliable and functional car that you have already paid off. Frugality helps you avoid compulsive shopping for things that you have to finance and pay over time even with interests. At the end of the day, you will find out that you must have paid more than double for the item. This too is a waste. Frugality makes you wise. If you need to buy any item or service, frugality will help you save money by making sure you compare prices from more sellers and dealers instead of merely buying from the first seller. It affords you the wisdom to research more about the product and make a better choice for less. You do not need a mansion with many rooms and features when you literally only sleep in one room and on one bed. You do not need a private jet and a helicopter when there are more economical ways of getting to your destination and saving the balance to support the many needy people around that you can empower to become successful men too; if you think you have excess money. The next time you have to spend money, kindly ask yourself these few questions: 'Do I really need this?' 'Can I live without this?' 'Will I die if I do not have this?' 'If I save or Invest this money, how much will it become in 5 years?' Etc.

Budget, Budget, Budget

Jesus taught his people to budget and said in Luke 14:28-30 (NIV) "Suppose one of you wants to build a tower. Won't you first sit down and estimate the cost to see if you have enough money to complete it? For if you lay the foundation and are not able to finish it, everyone who sees it will ridicule you, saying, 'This person began to build and wasn't able to finish.' Budgeting should become a habit of someone who applies frugality in his life. He must make sure he calculates the cost of every of his endeavors and not just financially but emotional and relationship costs. You should avoid engaging in acts you did not plan for, especially compulsive habits of aimless shopping. By budgeting, the great man has the ability to streamline his life and spending only to necessities and not luxury.

Put Money Last

We should not treat money as the most important thing in life. Money is a means to an end, and not the end in itself. In business, one should never invest in business only for the money aspect, but the service. Money will always come later. Selfless service to the community should be respected and taken seriously for any business endeavor. Great men would always respect the needs of their community and offer their services before expecting money and profits. Let us consider Jeff Bezos and what he does at Amazon.com. At the beginning, Amazon.com was not earning profits, but Jeff was busy trying to get customers and winning the competition, so he decided to push profits and money forward as a long-term goal.

Chapter Summary

1. Great men are not wasteful
2. Money does not control them
3. They do not believe money is everything but a means
4. They possess financial intelligence
5. They make their money work for them on autopilot
6. They cannot be bought with money
7. They know how to delay gratification
8. They are not overambitious
9. Greed does not rule them
10. They are not envious of richer people
11. They do not compete with other people
12. They do not support dangerous habits

Conclusion

I congratulate you for reading up to this page. I assume you have studied the 12 principles that made Jesus Christ successful as a great man on earth. I believe you are likely to apply some or all these principles to your life as you aspire to become a great man in your society. These principles are not strange, but they are vital to every man or woman who wishes to be successful in life. I also believe you have decided to discover, develop and deploy your God-given talents to the advancement of your society, and to fulfill your life's purpose and destiny.

I believe you can now perceive people in a positive light. You can now realize every person has both good and evil traits in them. When you dwell on people's positive side, the evil side weakens automatically. But the evil side of the person is fed with much attention from other people. We should learn how to focus on the positive values of people to enable them to become better. Praise anyone around you, who deserves praise. Encourage whoever does not deserve praise. Condemn the evil and immoral deeds of people but never condemn the people. Give everyone another chance because we are all capable of mistakes. Correct each other in love and never hate anyone.

What then shall we say to every living man or woman today? You have a choice either to remain an irrelevant person in your society or become a great man or woman. Our societies need more of its citizens to become and operate as great men and women to help create a balance between its majority and minority. Great people are the intermediaries between the rich and the poor in the society. They are the means by which the poor people get justice. The great men are the ones who bring the oppressors to justice by fighting injustice and segregation.

Considering the recent uprising in the American society resulting from police brutality towards the black man, the war against inequality and injustice has been rekindled and it needs every living person to join the fight. It is the duty of the great men to stand and fight for the equal rights of all people. This war is global and needs every morally correct person to join and show support.

You are as qualified as anyone else to become a great person in your locality and it is never too late to start. There are acts of injustice against other humans around the world by the second. But we have a handful of great men who counter all these acts. Your silence on global injustice only encourages the oppressor to harm more people. Look around you and find any act of injustice or oppression and if you observe something, say something! There is a platform that has helped in the war against injustice, the social media. Your cellphone is your reporting tool and prayer is your weapon.

When you overlook any deed of injustice and immorality around you, it is a confirmation that you have endorsed that as the new norm. Soon it might become your turn as the victim and then no one would come to your help. You might even think you are above the law, but you have forgotten about your extended family members who can get caught up in the same mess. I bid you wake up today and defend the innocent members of your society before it becomes too late.

About the Author

Pastor Juddie Udoh Passion is a preacher, teacher, and an inspirational writer. He writes from revelation knowledge and his goal is to bless his readers with heavenly principles for spiritual and secular success and excellence. He is a staunch believer in Jesus Christ and preaches the same to all his readers.

Pastor J. U. Passion's love for books made him start iPromosmedia LLC, specializing in media publishing and web development. He heads the team of experts in book publishing (books, magazines, newspapers, newsletters, desktop publishing and graphics design etc.) Including writing, formatting, editing, cover design, marketing, and promotions. He is also a computer support technician.

He is also a renewable energy consultant, he has many renewable energy projects in Africa including but not limited to building green & smart cities, green & smart buildings, green & smart mobile primary health care clinics, solar power systems, solar devices and empowering micro small to medium enterprises (MSMEs). He is a member of the Africa Clean Energy Group, Inc., FL. USA

He is the Senior Pastor of Uncommon Grace Ministries, Inc., Florida, USA and a father of 2, Sammie & Debbie.

Other Books by The Author

1. Acts (Deeds) of Greatness
2. Parable of Greatness
3. Parable of Fishing
4. How to become an MLK
5. How to become a Mandela
6. The Motherland Exodus (Back to Africa)
7. The Curse of The Melanocytes
8. Egalitarian Democracy
9. What-if It Is Written
10. The Manufacturing Economy
11. My Natural and Unwritten Laws
12. The Water Winning Formula

www.ingramcontent.com/pod-product-compliance
Lightning Source LLC
Chambersburg PA
CBHW070954080526
44587CB00015B/2306